Claim Models

Claim Models

Granular Forms and Machine Learning Forms

Special Issue Editor
Greg Taylor

MDPI • Basel • Beijing • Wuhan • Barcelona • Belgrade • Manchester • Tokyo • Cluj • Tianjin

Special Issue Editor
Greg Taylor
University of New South Wales
Australia

Editorial Office
MDPI
St. Alban-Anlage 66
4052 Basel, Switzerland

This is a reprint of articles from the Special Issue published online in the open access journal *Risks* (ISSN 2227-9091) (available at: https://www.mdpi.com/journal/risks/special_issues/learning_forms).

For citation purposes, cite each article independently as indicated on the article page online and as indicated below:

LastName, A.A.; LastName, B.B.; LastName, C.C. Article Title. *Journal Name* **Year**, *Article Number*, Page Range.

ISBN 978-3-03928-664-5 (Pbk)
ISBN 978-3-03928-665-2 (PDF)

© 2020 by the authors. Articles in this book are Open Access and distributed under the Creative Commons Attribution (CC BY) license, which allows users to download, copy and build upon published articles, as long as the author and publisher are properly credited, which ensures maximum dissemination and a wider impact of our publications.

The book as a whole is distributed by MDPI under the terms and conditions of the Creative Commons license CC BY-NC-ND.

Contents

About the Special Issue Editor vii

Greg Taylor
Risks Special Issue on "Granular Models and Machine Learning Models"
Reprinted from: *Risks* **2020**, *8*, 1, doi:10.3390/risks8010001 1

Massimo De Felice and Franco Moriconi
Claim Watching and Individual Claims Reserving Using Classification and Regression Trees
Reprinted from: *Risks* **2019**, *7*, 102, doi:10.3390/risks7040102 3

Francis Duval and Mathieu Pigeon
Individual Loss Reserving Using a Gradient Boosting-Based Approach
Reprinted from: *Risks* **2019**, *7*, 79, doi:10.3390/risks7030079 39

Kevin Kuo
DeepTriangle: A Deep Learning Approach to Loss Reserving
Reprinted from: *Risks* **2019**, *7*, 97, doi:10.3390/risks7030097 57

Jacky H. L. Poon
Penalising Unexplainability in Neural Networks for Predicting Payments per Claim Incurred
Reprinted from: *Risks* **2019**, *7*, 95, doi:10.3390/risks7030095 69

Greg Taylor
Loss Reserving Models: Granular and Machine Learning Forms
Reprinted from: *Risks* **2019**, *7*, 82, doi:10.3390/risks7030082 81

About the Special Issue Editor

Greg Taylor Adjunct Professor of Risk and Actuarial Studies, University of New South Wales, holds a Ph.D. in Actuarial Mathematicsand a Ph.D. in Theoretical Physics both from from Macquarie University, Sydney, Australia. He is a Fellow of the Institute and Faculty of Actuaries (U.K.), a Fellow of the Institute of Actuaries of Australia, a Corresponding Member of the Swiss Association of Actuaries, and a Fellow of the Institute of Mathematics and Its Applications. He has been recognized as an Officer of the Order of Australia for service to the nation, and was awarded the Gold Medal of the Institute of Actuaries of Australia and the Finlaison Medal of the Institute and Faculty of Actuaries. He worked as an actuary in industry over the 44 years from 1962 to 1968 and 1977 to 2013, and spent the intervening period as an academic. Of the 44 years in industry, 35 were spent as a consulting actuary, mainly concerned with general insurance. He has published a number of books and numerous papers and contributed chapters.

Editorial

Risks Special Issue on "Granular Models and Machine Learning Models"

Greg Taylor

School of Risk and Actuarial Studies, University of New South Wales, Kensington, NSW 2052, Australia; greg_taylor60@hotmail.com

Received: 8 December 2019; Accepted: 13 December 2019; Published: 30 December 2019

It is probably fair to date loss reserving by means of claim modelling from the late 1960s. For much of the 50 years since then, the models have either remained algebraically simple, or have incrementally proceeded to greater algebraic complexity. Much of the limitation on model sophistication has derived from computing limitations.

As computing power has increased, so has model complexity and sophistication. At some point on this journey, the modelling of the claim process of individual claims in detail (**granular modelling (GM)**) became feasible. More recently, **machine learning (ML)** has increasingly found its way into the literature. Again, this may (though not necessarily will) target individual claims.

The two approaches stand in stark contrast with each other in at least one respect. In my own contribution to the present volume, I refer to them as the Watchmaker (GM) and the Oracle (ML), the one being concerned with ever more detailed and minute modelling, and the other with incisive generalizations about data on the basis of reasoning that may be obscure or even impenetrable.

The appearance of two (relatively) new approaches to the estimation of individual claim loss reserves immediately creates a tension between them, with natural questions about their relative performances. But the issue is greater than this. There are also questions about the performance of new versus old models.

I have no doubt that some of these new approaches will prove useful in future, and quite possibly dominate all others. For the present, however, their status is, in my view, unproven. The research record contains a number of papers in this field, but some of them consist of an application to a single dataset with little in the way of general conclusions or indication of the extent to which the results could be extrapolated to other datasets.

The consequence is a fragmented research record, leaving open questions about the general applicability of GM and ML. Some of the (to my mind) landmark questions requiring answer are the following.

1. **Modelling of individual claims.** This is possible with GM and ML. However, it is a statistical truism that enlargement of the volume of data used does not necessarily increase predictive power. Indeed, in Section 8.2 of my own contribution to this volume, I give an example where it will not. So, can we identify the circumstances in which the use of individual claims is likely to bring predictive benefit?
2. **Complexity.** One might reasonably guess that the answer to the previous question will be somehow related to the complexity of the dataset under analysis. In short, datasets with simple algebraic structures have simple methods of analysis, and complex datasets have more complex methods, and possibly individual claims. So, can we design a metric of data complexity (perhaps based on relative entropy or similar) that could be used to triage datasets?
3. **Predictive gain.** In cases where some predictive gain is found, say reduced prediction error or more granular reserving or some other form of GM/ML supremacy, what exactly is the gain

in quantitative terms, and are there any general indications of the circumstances in which it might occur?
4. **Interpretability.** Explainable neural nets (NNs) have entered the literature. These structured NN outputs so as to increase their interpretability. Even so, the results are not always quite transparent. Can we define alternative constraints in the form of output so as to enhance interpretability further?
5. **Interpretability (continued).** In any case, to what extent is interpretability paramount? Can we define circumstances in which it is essential, and others where it does not matter?

The present volume commences with two articles on loss reserving at the individual claim level, in each case using a form of machine learning. De Felice and Moriconi (2019) use CART (Classification And Regression Trees) together with some granular features, whereas Duval and Pigeon (2019) use gradient boosting.

These are followed by two articles on neural networks. Kuo (2019) apples deep learning to claim triangles, but with multi-triangle input and other input features. Then, Poon (2019) is concerned with the issue of interpretability, applying an unexplainability penalty to the neural network.

Finally, my own contribution (Taylor 2019) discusses the merits and demerits of GM and ML models, and compares the two families.

Funding: This research received funding assistance from the Australian Research Council, grant number LP130100723.

Conflicts of Interest: The author declares no conflict of interest.

References

De Felice, Massimo, and Franco Moriconi. 2019. Claim Watching and Individual Claims Reserving Using Classification and Regression Trees. *Risks* 7: 102. [CrossRef]
Duval, Francis, and Mathieu Pigeon. 2019. Individual Loss Reserving Using a Gradient Boosting-Based Approach. *Risks* 7: 79.
Kuo, Kevin. 2019. DeepTriangle: A Deep Learning Approach to Loss Reserving. *Risks* 7: 97. [CrossRef]
Poon, Jacky HL. 2019. Penalising Unexplainability in Neural Networks for Predicting Payments per Claim Incurred. *Risks* 7: 95. [CrossRef]
Taylor, Greg. 2019. Loss Reserving Models: Granular and Machine Learning Forms. *Risks* 7: 82. [CrossRef]

© 2019 by the author. Licensee MDPI, Basel, Switzerland. This article is an open access article distributed under the terms and conditions of the Creative Commons Attribution (CC BY) license (http://creativecommons.org/licenses/by/4.0/).

Article

Claim Watching and Individual Claims Reserving Using Classification and Regression Trees

Massimo De Felice [1] and Franco Moriconi [2,3,*]

[1] Department of Statitistical Sciences, Sapienza University of Rome, 00185 Rome, Italy; massimo.defelice@alef.it
[2] Department of Economics, University of Perugia, 06123 Perugia, Italy
[3] Alef—Advanced Laboratory Economics and Finance, 00198 Rome, Italy
* Correspondence: franco.moriconi1@unipg.it

Received: 21 August 2019; Accepted: 2 October 2019; Published: 12 October 2019

Abstract: We present an approach to individual claims reserving and claim watching in general insurance based on classification and regression trees (CART). We propose a compound model consisting of a *frequency* section, for the prediction of events concerning reported claims, and a *severity* section, for the prediction of paid and reserved amounts. The formal structure of the model is based on a set of probabilistic assumptions which allow the provision of sound statistical meaning to the results provided by the CART algorithms. The multiperiod predictions required for claims reserving estimations are obtained by compounding one-period predictions through a simulation procedure. The resulting dynamic model allows the joint modeling of the case reserves, which usually yields useful predictive information. The model also allows predictions under a double-claim regime, i.e., when two different types of compensation can be required by the same claim. Several explicit numerical examples are provided using motor insurance data. For a large claims portfolio we derive an aggregate reserve estimate obtained as the sum of individual reserve estimates and we compare the result with the classical chain-ladder estimate. Backtesting exercises are also proposed concerning event predictions and claim-reserve estimates.

Keywords: individual claims reserving; claim watching; classification and regression trees; machine learning

---

1. Introduction

In the settlement process of a general insurance claims portfolio we denote as *claim watching* the insurer's activityconsisting of monitoring and controlling the cost development at single-claim level. Claim watching encompasses prediction of specific events regarding individual claims that can be relevant for cost development and could be influenced by possible appropriate management actions. Obviously, the estimation of the ultimate cost, hence the *individual claims reserving*, is also a typical claim watching activity. Early-warning systems at single-claim or group-of-claims level can be also included.

In this paper, we propose a machine-learning approach to claim watching, and individual claims reserving, using a prediction model based on the classification and regression trees (CART). The paper is largely based on a path-breaking article produced in 2016 by Mario Wüthrich (Wüthrich 2016) where individual claims reserving is addressed by CART techniques. The method proposed by Wüthrich was restricted "*for pedagogical reasons*" to the prediction of events and the estimation of the number of payments related to individual claims. We extend Wüthrich's paper providing a so-called *frequency-severity model* where claim amounts paid are also considered. Moreover, we enlarge the set of the response and explanatory variables of the model to allow prediction under a double-claim regime, i.e., when two different types of compensation can be required by the same claim. This multi-regime extension enables us to provide meaningful applications to Italian motor insurance claims data. We also propose a further enhancement of the CART approach allowing the joint dynamic modeling of the case reserves, which usually yield useful predictive information.

The claim watching idea and a related frequency-severity model based on CARTs were introduced and developed in D'Agostino et al. (2018) and large part of the material presented here was already contained in that paper.

According to a point of view proposed in Hiabu et al. (2015), a possible inclusion of a granular data approach in claims reserving could be provided by extending classical aggregate methods, adding more model structure to include underlying effects which are supposed to emerge at an individual claim level. In Hiabu et al. (2015) this approach is illustrated by referring to a series of extensions of the Double Chain-Ladder (DCL) model, originated in Verral et al. (2010) and developed in successive papers, (see e.g., Martínez-Miranda et al. 2011, 2012, 2013). Approaches to claims reserving recently proposed based on embedding a classical actuarial model in a neural net (see e.g., Gabrielli et al. 2018; Wüthrich and Merz 2019) could also be interpreted as going in a similar "top-down" direction. A different path is followed in this paper. We use the large model flexibility provided by machine-learning methods for directly modeling individual claim histories. In this approach model assumptions are specified at granular level and are, in some sense, the minimal required to guarantee a sound statistical meaning to results provided by the powerful algorithms currently available. This allows implantation of claim watching activities which can be considered even more general than traditional claims reserving.

This paper, however, has several limitations. In particular, only point estimates of the ultimate claim cost are considered and the important problem of prediction uncertainty is not addressed, yet. Moreover, these cost estimates do not fully include underwriting year inflation, then an appropriate model should be added to this aim. Therefore, the present paper should be considered to be only a starting point in applying CARTs to claims reserving and claims handling. By analogy, one could say that in introducing machine learning to individual reserving data this paper is playing the same role as Verral et al. (2010) was playing in DCL: many improvements and developments should follow.

The present paper is composed of two parts. In the first part one-period prediction problems are considered. Prediction problems typical in claim watching and individual claims reserving are presented in Section 2 and notation and a basic assumption (i.e., the dependence of the prediction functions on the observation time-lag) are introduced in Section 3. In Section 4 we describe the general structure of the frequency-severity approach, providing details on the model assumptions for both the model components. The structure of the feature space, both for static and dynamic variables, is described in Section 5 and the organization of data required for the CART calibrations is illustrated in Section 6. In Section 7 the use of classification trees for the frequency prediction, and regression trees for (conditional) severity predictions is illustrated. In Section 8 a first extensive example of one-year predictions for a claims portfolio in Italian motor insurance is presented using the rpart routine implemented in R. The results of the CART calibration are discussed in detail and a possible use of event predictions for early warning is illustrated.

The second part of the paper considers multiperiod predictions and includes numerical examples and backtesting exercises. In Section 9 we consider multiperiod predictions and describe the properties required for deriving multiyear forecasts by compounding one-year forecasts. In Section 10 a simulation approach to multiperiod forecasts is also presented and additional assumptions allowing the joint dynamic modeling of the case reserves are discussed. A first numerical example of multiperiod prediction of a single-claim cost is also provided. Section 11 is devoted to numerical examples of applications to a large claims portfolio in motor insurance and to some backtesting exercises providing insights into the predictive performance of our CART approach. We first illustrate backtesting results for predictions of one-year event occurrences useful for claim watching. Finally, a typical claim reserving exercise is provided, composed of two steps. In a first step the individual reserve estimate is derived by simulation for all the claims in the portfolio and the resulting total reserve, after the addition of an IBNYR (*incurred but not yet reported*) reserve estimate, is compared with the classical chain-ladder reserve, estimated on aggregate payments at portfolio level (an ancillary model for IBNYR reserves is outlined in Appendix A). Since we perform these estimates on data deprived of the last calendar year observations, we analyze the predictive accuracy of the CART approach with respect to the chain-ladder approach by comparing the realized aggregate payments in the "first next diagonal" with those predicted by the two methods. Some conclusions are presented in Section 12.

Part I. One-period Predictions

2. A First Look at the Problem and the Model

Let us consider the claim portfolio of a given line of business of a non-life insurer. We are interested in the individual claim settlement processes of this portfolio. For example, for a given claim $\mathcal{C}$ in the portfolio, we would like to answer questions like these:

(a) What is the probability that $\mathcal{C}$ is closed in the next year?
(b) What is the probability that a lawyer will be involved in the settlement of $\mathcal{C}$ in two years?
(c) What is the expectation of a payment in respect of $\mathcal{C}$ in the next year?
(d) What is the expectation of the total claim payments in respect of $\mathcal{C}$ until finalization?

In general, we will refer to the activity of dealing with this kind of questions as *claim watching*. In particular, question (b) could be relevant in a possible early-warning system, while questions as (c) and (d) are more concerned with *individual claims reserving*. The classical *claims reserving*, i.e., the estimation of the outstanding loss liabilities aggregate over the entire portfolio, could be obtained by summing all the individual claim reserves with some corrections due to non-modeled effects (typically, reserve for IBNYR claims).

For a specified claim $\mathcal{C}$ in the portfolio, a typical claim watching question at time t can be formulated as a prediction problem with the form:

$$\mathbb{E}\left[Y_{t+\tau}^{(\mathcal{C})}\middle|\mathcal{F}_t\right] = \mu\left(x_t^{(\mathcal{C})}\right), \quad \tau > 0, \tag{1}$$

where:

- $\mathcal{F}_t$ denotes the information available at time t,
- the vector $x_t^{(\mathcal{C})} \in \mathcal{X}$ is the *claim feature* (also *covariates, explanatory variables, independent variables,* ...), which is observed up to time t, i.e., is $\mathcal{F}_t$-measurable,
- $\mu : \mathcal{X} \to \mathbb{R}$ is the *prediction function*,
- $Y_{t+\tau}^{(\mathcal{C})}$ is the *response variable* (or *dependent variable*).

Referring to the previous examples, the response in (1) can be specified as follows:

(a) $Y_{t+\tau}^{(\mathcal{C})}$ is the indicator function of the event $\{\mathcal{C}$ is closed at time $t+\tau\}$ (with $\tau = 1$),
(b) $Y_{t+\tau}^{(\mathcal{C})}$ is the indicator function of $\{\mathcal{C}$ will involve a lawyer by the time $t+\tau\}$ (with $\tau = 2$),
(c) $Y_{t+\tau}^{(\mathcal{C})}$ is the random variable denoting the amount paid in respect of $\mathcal{C}$ at time $t+\tau$ (with $\tau = 1$),
(d) $Y_{t+\tau}^{(\mathcal{C})}$ is the random variable denoting the cumulated paid amount in respect of $\mathcal{C}$ at time $t+\tau$ (with $\tau \to \infty$).

The response and the feature can be both quantitative or qualitative variables and we do not assume for the moment a particular structure for the prediction function μ, which must be estimated from the data. Usually, the prediction model (1) is referred to as *regression* model if the response is a quantitative variable and *classification* model if the response is qualitative (categorical). The prediction function is named, accordingly, as *regression* or *classifier* function[1].

Questions such as (a) and (b) involve prediction of events while questions such as (c) and (d) concern prediction of paid amounts. With some abuse of actuarial jargon, we will refer to a prediction model for event occurrences as a *frequency* model. Similarly, we will refer to a prediction model for paid amounts as a *severity* model. Then, altogether, we need a *frequency-severity* model. We will develop a frequency-severity model for claim watching with a *conditional* severity component that is the paid amounts are predicted conditionally on the payment is made. This is because the probability distribution of a paid amount, with a discrete mass in 0, is better modeled by separate recognition of the mass and the remainder of the distribution (assumed continuous).

Remark 1. *A model with such a structure can be also referred to as a cascaded model, see Taylor (2019) for a discussion of this kind of models. This model structure also bears some resemblance to Double Chain-Ladder (DCL), see Martínez-Miranda et al. (2012). In DCL a micro-model of the claims generating process is first introduced to predict the reported number of claims. Future payments are then predicted through a delay function and a severity model. In DCL, however, individual information is assumed to be "(in practice often) unobservable" and the micro-model is only aimed to derive a suitable reserving model for aggregate data. In this paper, instead, extensive individual information is assumed to be always available and each individual claim is identifiable. Moreover, we are interested in both claim watching and individual claims reserving, aggregate reserving being a possible byproduct of the approach.*

To deal with the prediction problems both in the frequency and the severity component we shall use the classification and regression trees (CART) techniques, namely classification trees for the frequency section and regression trees for the severity section. One of the main advantages of CART methods is the large modeling flexibility (for aggregate claims reserving methods with a good degree of model flexibility though not using machine learning, see e.g., Pešta and Okhrin 2014). Carts can deal with any sort of structured and unstructured information, an underlying structural form of the prediction function μ can be learned from the data, many explanatory variables can be used, both quantitative and qualitative and observed at different dates. Moreover, the interpretability of results is generally allowed. As methods for providing expectations, CARTs can also be referred to as *prediction trees*.

3. Notation and Basic Assumptions

The notation used in this paper is essentially the same as in Wüthrich (2016). For simplicity sake we model the claim settlement process using an annual time grid. If allowed by the available data, a discrete time grid with a shorter time step (semester, quarter, month, ...) could be used.

Accident year. For a given line of business in non-life insurance, let us consider a claims portfolio containing observations at the current date on the claims occurred during the last I accident years (ay). The accident years are indexed as $i = 1, \ldots, I$. Then we are at time (calendar year) $t = I$.

Reporting delay. For each accident year i, claims may have been observed with a *reporting delay* (rd) $j = 0, 1, \ldots$. A claim with accident year i and reporting delay j will have reporting date $i + j$. As usual, we assume that there exists a maximum possible delay $J \geq 0$.

---

[1] According to the logical foundations of probability theory, as stated by Bruno de Finetti in the 1930s mainly using the Italian language, the word corresponding to the English *prediction* is *previsione* (*prévision* in French) and not *predizione*. As strongly stated by de Finetti, *previsione* refers to *providing expectation*, while *predizione* refers to *providing certainty*, which obviously is possible only in a deterministic framework. A prediction problem can have a very general nature. Formulation (1) is only a particular, though important, specification. Usually prediction is also referred to as *forecast* or *foresight*.

Claims identification. Each claim is identified by a claim code cc. For each block (i,j) there are $N_{i,j}$ claims and we denote by $v = 1, \ldots, N_{i,j}$ the index numbering the claims in block (i,j); the v-th claim in (i,j) is denoted by $C_{i,j}^{(v)}$.

IBNYR claims. Because of the possible reporting delay, at a given date t we can have *incurred but not yet reported* (IBNYR) claims. Since there is a maximal delay J, at the current date the IBNYR claims are those with delay $j > (I-i) \wedge J$. The maximum observed reporting delay is $(I-1) \wedge J$.

Remark 2. *At time I, claims with $j \leq I - i$ can be closed or reported but not settled (RBNS). We can estimate a reserve required for these claims. For the IBNYR reserve estimate a specific reserving model is needed (see Appendix A).*

Predictions in the claim settlement process. For given i, j, v, the claim settlement process of $C_{i,j}^{(v)}$ is defined on the calendar dates $i+j$, $i+j+1$, $i+j+2$, ... Let us denote by:

- $X_{i,j|k}^{(v)}$ a generic random variable, possibly multidimensional, involved in the claim settlement process of $C_{i,j}^{(v)}$ and observed at time $t = i+j+k$, for $k \in \mathbb{N}_0$,
- $\ell := j + k = t - i$ the *time-lag* of $X_{i,j|k}^{(v)}$.

Using this notation, the prediction problem (1) for $\tau = 1$ is reformulated as follows:

$$\mathbb{E}\left[Y_{\underbrace{i,j|t-(i+j)+1}_{\text{date } t+1}}^{(v)} \middle| \mathcal{F}_{i+j+k}\right] = \mu\left(x_{\underbrace{i,j|t-(i+j)}_{\text{date } t}}^{(v)}\right), \qquad (2)$$

where the claim feature $x_{i,j|t-(i+j)}^{(v)} \in \mathcal{X}$ is $\mathcal{F}_{i+j+k}$-measurable, $\mu : \mathcal{X} \to \mathbb{R}$, and the response is possibly multidimensional. In the rest of the paper the prediction function μ will refer solely to one-year forecast problems. Multiyear prediction problems will be treated compounding one-year predictions.

To give some statistical structure to the prediction model, we make the following basic assumption on the prediction function:

(H0) *At any date t the one-year prediction function $\mu\left(x_{i,j|t-(i+j)}^{(v)}\right)$ depends only on the time-lag $\ell = t - i$. i.e.,:*

$$\mu_{t-i} : \mathcal{X} \to \mathbb{R}, \qquad x_{i,j|t-(i+j)}^{(v)} \mapsto \mu_{t-i}\left(x_{i,j|t-(i+j)}^{(v)}\right).$$

Then the μ_{t-i} function is independent of v and is applied to all the features with the same time-lag $\ell = t - i$, providing the expectation of $Y_{i,j|t-(i+j)+1}^{(v)}$ (which has time-lag $\ell + 1$).

Under assumption (H0) we can build statistical samples of observed pairs feature-response which can be used to derive an estimate of unobserved responses based on observed features.

In what follows it will be often convenient to rewrite the prediction problem using the k index. Since $t = i + j + k$ expression (2), taking account of assumption (H0), takes the form:

$$\mathbb{E}\left[Y_{i,j|k+1}^{(v)} \middle| \mathcal{F}_{i+j+k}\right] = \mu_{j+k}\left(x_{i,j|k}^{(v)}\right). \qquad (3)$$

4. The General Structure of the Frequency-Severity Model

To give a formal characterization of the entire claim settlement process we have to recall that $N_{i,j}$ denotes the number of claims occurred in accident year i reported in calendar year $i + j$. Then in a general setting we let the relevant indexes vary as follows:

$$i = 1, \ldots, I, \quad j = 0, \ldots, J, \quad v \in \mathbb{N}_1, \quad k \in \mathbb{N}_0,$$

and we consider also $N_{i,j}$ as a stochastic process.

4.1. Frequency and Severity Response Variables

The peculiarity of the frequency model is that the response variables $Y_{i,j|k}^{(v)}$ are defined as a multi-event, which is a vector of 0–1 random variables. Precisely, for all values of i,j,v and k we assume that a frequency-type response at time $i+j+k$ for the claim $C_{i,j}^{(v)}$ takes the form:

$$F_{i,j|k}^{(v)} = \left({}_h F_{i,j|k}^{(v)},\ h=1,\ldots,d\right)' \quad \text{with} \quad {}_h F_{i,j|k}^{(v)} \in \{0,1\},\ h=1,\ldots,d.$$

As concerning severity, we shall assume that in the claim settlement process two different kinds of claim payments are possible, say type-1 and type-2 payments. Then we shall indicate with $S1_{i,j|k}^{(v)}$ and $S2_{i,j|k}^{(v)}$ the random variable denoting a claim payment of type 1 and type 2, respectively, made at time $i+j+k$. For all values of i,j,v and k, a severity-type response for $C_{i,j}^{(v)}$ will be denoted in general as $S_{i,j|k}^{(v)}$, which will be specified as $S1_{i,j|k}^{(v)}$ or $S2_{i,j|k}^{(v)}$ according to a type-1 or type-2 cash flow is to be predicted. We shall also denote by $\tilde{S}1_{i,j|k}^{(v)}$ and $\tilde{S}2_{i,j|k}^{(v)}$) the binary variables:

$$\tilde{S}1_{i,j|k}^{(v)} = \mathbf{1}_{\{S1_{i,j|k}^{(v)} \neq 0\}},\quad \tilde{S}2_{i,j|k}^{(v)} = \mathbf{1}_{\{S2_{i,j|k}^{(v)} \neq 0\}},$$

i.e., the indicator of the event {A claim payment of type 1 for $C_{i,j}^{(v)}$ is made at time $i+j+k$} and {A claim payment of type 2 for $C_{i,j}^{(v)}$ is made at time $i+j+k$}, respectively.

Remark 3. *The assumption of multiple payment types will be necessary in our applications to Italian Motor Third Party Liability (MTPL) data. Essentially, in Italian MTPL incurred claims can be handled, according to their characteristics, under (at least) two different regimes: direct compensation ("CARD" regime) and indirect compensation ("NoCARD" regime). Case reserves in the two regimes are different and a claim can activate one or both, as well as can change regime. In our numerical examples we shall denote NoCARD and CARD payments/reserves as type-1 and type-2 payments/reserves, respectively.*

The following model assumptions extend the set of assumptions used in Wüthrich (2016).

4.2. Model Assumptions

Let $(\Omega, \mathcal{F}, \mathbb{P}, \mathbb{F})$ be a filtered probability space with filtration $\mathbb{F} = (\mathcal{F}_t)_{t \in \mathbb{N}_0}$ such that for $i = 1,\ldots,I$, $j = 0,\ldots,J$, $v = 1,\ldots,N_{i,j}$, $k \in \mathbb{N}_0$, the process $(N_{i,j})_{i,j}$ is $\mathbb{F}$-adapted for $t = i+j$ and all the processes:

$$(F_{i,j|k}^{(v)})_{i,j,k,v},\quad (S1_{i,j|k}^{(v)})_{i,j,k,v},\quad (S2_{i,j|k}^{(v)})_{i,j,k,v},$$

are $\mathbb{F}$-adapted for $t = i+j+k$. We make the following assumptions:

(H1) The processes $(N_{i,j})_{i,j}$, $(F_{i,j|k}^{(v)})_{i,j,k,v}$, $(S1_{i,j|k}^{(v)})_{i,j,k,v}$ and $(S2_{i,j|k}^{(v)})_{i,j,k,v}$ are independent.

(H2) The random variables in $(N_{i,j})_{i,j}$, $(F_{i,j|k}^{(v)})_{i,j,k,v}$, $(S1_{i,j|k}^{(v)})_{i,j,k,v}$ and $(S2_{i,j|k}^{(v)})_{i,j,k,v}$ for different accident years are independent.

(H3) The processes $(F_{i,j|k}^{(v)})_k$, $(S1_{i,j|k}^{(v)})_{i,j,k,v}$ and $(S2_{i,j|k}^{(v)})_{i,j,k,v}$ for different reporting delays j and different claims v are independent.

(H4) The conditional distribution of $F_{i,j|k}^{(v)}$ is the d-dimensional Bernoulli:

$$F_{i,j|k+1}^{(v)} | \mathcal{F}_{i+j+k} \sim d\text{-Bernoulli}\left(p_{j+k}^{(f)}(x_{i,j|k}^{(v)})\right),$$

with $\boldsymbol{f} = (f_1, \ldots, f_d), f_1, \ldots, f_d \in \{0, 1\}$ and where $x_{i,j|k}^{(v)} \in \mathcal{X}$ is the $\mathcal{F}_{i+j+k}$-measurable frequency feature of $C_{i,j|k}^{(v)}$ and $p_{j+k}^{(f)} : \mathcal{X} \mapsto [0, 1]^{2^d}$ is a probability function, i.e.:

$$\sum_{f_1, \ldots, f_d \in \{0,1\}} p_{j+k}^{(f)}(x_{i,j|k}^{(v)}) = 1.$$

(H5) For the conditional distribution of $S1_{i,j|k}^{(v)} | (S1_{i,j|k}^{(v)} = 1)$ and $S2_{i,j|k}^{(v)} | (S2_{i,j|k}^{(v)} = 1)$ one has:

$$\begin{aligned} S1_{i,j|k+1}^{(v)} \Big| \left(\tilde{S1}_{i,j|k+1}^{(v)} = 1\right) &\sim \mathcal{N}\left(\tilde{\mu}_{j+k}^{(1)}(\tilde{x}_{i,j|k}^{(v)}), \sigma_1^2\right), \\ S2_{i,j|k+1}^{(v)} \Big| \left(\tilde{S2}_{i,j|k+1}^{(v)} = 1\right) &\sim \mathcal{N}\left(\tilde{\mu}_{j+k}^{(2)}(\tilde{x}_{i,j|k}^{(v)}), \sigma_2^2\right), \end{aligned} \quad (4)$$

where $\tilde{x}_{i,j|k}^{(v)} \in \mathcal{X}$ is the $\mathcal{F}_{i+j+k}$-measurable severity feature of $C_{i,j|k}^{(v)}$.

Assumption (H4) implies that for every claims $C_{i,j|k}^{(v)}$ reported at time $i + j + k$:

$$\mathbb{P}\left[{}_1F_{i,j|k+1}^{(v)} = f_1, \ldots, {}_dF_{i,j|k+1}^{(v)} = f_d \Big| \mathcal{F}_{i+j+k} \right] = p_{j+k}^{(f)}\left(x_{i,j|k}^{(v)}\right) \geq 0, \quad (5)$$

and:

$$\sum_{f_1, \ldots, f_d \in \{0,1\}} p_{j+k}^{(f)}\left(x_{i,j|k}^{(v)}\right) = 1.$$

Therefore, there exists an $\mathcal{F}_{i+j+k}$-measurable frequency feature $x_{i,j|k}^{(v)}$ which determines the conditional probability of each (binary) component of the response variable. Expression (5) provides the specification of the prediction problem (3) for the frequency model.

Similarly, assumption (4) implies that for every claims $C_{i,j|k}^{(v)}$ reported at time $i + j + k$:

$$\begin{aligned} \mathbb{E}\left[S1_{i,j|k+1}^{(v)} \Big| \mathcal{F}_{i+j+k}, \left(\tilde{S1}_{i,j|k+1}^{(v)} = 1\right) \right] &= \tilde{\mu}_{j+k}^{(1)}\left(\tilde{x}_{i,j|k}^{(v)}\right), \\ \mathbb{E}\left[S2_{i,j|k+1}^{(v)} \Big| \mathcal{F}_{i+j+k}, \left(\tilde{S2}_{i,j|k+1}^{(v)} = 1\right) \right] &= \tilde{\mu}_{j+k}^{(2)}\left(\tilde{x}_{i,j|k}^{(v)}\right). \end{aligned} \quad (6)$$

Then there exists an $\mathcal{F}_{i+j+k}$-measurable severity feature $\tilde{x}_{i,j|k}^{(v)}$ which determines the conditional expectation of the cash flows $S1_{i,j|k}^{(v)}$ and $S2_{i,j|k}^{(v)}$. The previous assumptions specify a compound frequency-severity model. From (6):

$$\begin{aligned} \mathbb{E}\left[S1_{i,j|k+1}^{(v)} \Big| \mathcal{F}_{i+j+k} \right] &= \tilde{\mu}_{j+k}^{(1)}\left(\tilde{x}_{i,j|k}^{(v)}\right) \mathbb{P}\left[\tilde{S1}_{i,j|k+1}^{(v)} = 1 \Big| \mathcal{F}_{i+j+k} \right], \\ \mathbb{E}\left[S2_{i,j|k+1}^{(v)} \Big| \mathcal{F}_{i+j+k} \right] &= \tilde{\mu}_{j+k}^{(2)}\left(\tilde{x}_{i,j|k}^{(v)}\right) \mathbb{P}\left[\tilde{S2}_{i,j|k+1}^{(v)} = 1 \Big| \mathcal{F}_{i+j+k} \right]. \end{aligned} \quad (7)$$

If the indicators $\tilde{S1}_{i,j|k+1}^{(v)}$ and $\tilde{S2}_{i,j|k+1}^{(v)}$ have been included in the response vector for the frequency model, the corresponding probabilities are provided by (5) and the severity expectations are then obtained by this compound model. Expression (7) provides the specification of the prediction problem (3) for the (two types of) severity model in the framework of this compound model.

Remark 4. *As regards model assumptions:*

- *The independence assumptions (H1), (H2) and (H3) were taken to receive a not too much complex model. In particular, assumptions in (H1) are necessary to obtain compound distributions, assumptions in (H3) allow the modeling of variables of individual claims independently for different v.*

- However, the specified model is rather general as regarding the prediction functions p and $\widetilde{\mu}$ in (5) and (6). These functions at the moment are fully non-parametric and can have any form. In the following sections we will show how these functions can be calibrated with machine-learning methods provided by CARTs.
- The value of the variance parameters σ_1^2, σ_2^2 in (4) is irrelevant since the normality assumption is used in this paper only to support the sum of squared errors (SSE) minimization for the calibration of the regression trees. The value of the variance is irrelevant in this minimization.
- Our model assumptions concern only one-year forecasting (from time t to $t + 1$). Under proper conditions multiyear predictions can be obtained by compounding one-period predictions. This will be illustrated in Section 9.

4.3. Equivalent One-Dimensional Formulation of Frequency Responses

The frequency prediction problem can be reformulated equivalently by replacing the d-dimensional binary random variables $F_{i,j|k+1}^{(v)}$ by the one-dimensional random variable:

$$W_{i,j|k+1}^{(v)} = \sum_{h=1}^{d} 2^{h-1} {}_h F_{i,j|k+1}^{(v)} \in \{0, \ldots, 2^d - 1\}. \tag{8}$$

In this case, assumption (H4) is replaced by:

(H4′) *For the conditional distribution of $W_{i,j|k}^{(v)}$ one has:*

$$W_{i,j|k+1}^{(v)} | \mathcal{F}_{i+j+k} \sim \text{Categorical}\left(p_{j+k}^{(w)}(x_{i,j|k}^{(v)})\right),$$

where $p_{j+k}^{(w)} : \mathcal{X} \mapsto [0,1]^{2^d}$ is a probability function, i.e.:

$$\sum_{w=0}^{2^d-1} p_{j+k}^{(w)}(x_{i,j|k}^{(v)}) = 1.$$

Expression (5) is then rewritten accordingly:

$$\mathbb{P}\left[W_{i,j|k+1}^{(v)} = w \middle| \mathcal{F}_{i+j+k}\right] = p_{j+k}^{(w)}\left(x_{i,j|k}^{(v)}\right) \geq 0, \quad w = 0, \ldots, 2^d - 1. \tag{9}$$

In the numerical examples presented in this paper we shall use formulation (8) for the frequency response since the R package rpart we use in these examples, multidimensional responses are not supported.

5. Characterizing the Feature Space

Given the high modeling flexibility of CARTs, the feature space $\mathcal{X}$ in our applications can be very large and with rather general characteristics. In the following discussion we refer to the frequency features $x_{i,j|k}^{(v)}$; the same properties hold for the severity features $\widetilde{x}_{i,j|k}^{(v)}$. Typically, for all i, j, v, k the feature $x_{i,j|k}^{(v)}$ is a vector with a large number of components. The feature components can be categorical, ordered or numerical. As pointed out by Taylor et al. (2008) the concept of static and dynamic variable is also important when considering the feature components.

Static variables. These are components of $x_{i,j|k}^{(v)}$ which remain unchanged during the life of the claim $\mathcal{C}_{i,j}^{(v)}$. Typical static variables are the claim code cc (categorical), the accident year i and the reporting delay j (ordered).

Dynamic variables. These feature components may randomly change over time. This implies that in general we have to understand $x_{i,j|k}^{(v)}$ as containing information on $\mathcal{C}_{i,j}^{(v)}$ up to time $i + j + k$. For example, the entire payment history of the claim up to time $i+j+k$ may be included in $x^{(v)}_{i,j|k}$. Therefore, when time passes more and more information is collected and the dimension of $x^{(v)}_{i,j|k}$ increases.

Typical examples of dynamic feature components are the categorical variable $\tilde{S1}^{(v)}_{i,j|k}$ which can take different 0-1 values for $k \in \mathbb{N}_0$, or the numerical variable $\tilde{S2}^{(v)}_{i,j|k}$ which can take different values in $\mathbb{R}$ for $k \in \mathbb{N}_0$. The categorical variable:

$$Z^{(v)}_{i,j|k} = \mathbf{1}_{\{C^{(v)}_{i,j} \text{ is closed at time } i+j+k\}},$$

is better modeled as a dynamic variable, since we observe that a closed claim can be reopened.

At time $i+j+k$ the structure of feature $x^{(v)}_{i,j|k}$ of $C^{(v)}_{i,j}$ can be expressed as:

$$x^{(v)}_{i,j|k} = \left(A^{(v)}_{i,j}, B^{(v)}_{i,j|0}, \ldots, B^{(v)}_{i,j|k} \right)', \qquad (10)$$

where:

- $A^{(v)}_{i,j}$ is a column vector of static variables,
- $B^{(v)}_{i,j|h}$, $h = 0, \ldots, k$, is a column vector of dynamic variables observed in year $i+j+h$.

Following Wüthrich (2016), if $j > 0$ for each variable in $B^{(v)}_{i,j|0}$ the observed value is preceded by a sequence of j zeros. An alternative choice could be to insert "NA" instead of zeros, provided that we are able to control how the CART routine used for calibration handles missing values in predictors.

From (10) one can say that $x^{(v)}_{i,j|k}$ provides the feature history of $C^{(v)}_{i,j}$ up to time $i+j+k$, while the vector $B^{(v)}_{i,j|k+1}$ provides its development in the next year $i+j+k+1$.

For example, for claim $C^{(v)}_{i,1}$ the feature at time $i+2$ could be specified as:

$$x^{(v)}_{i,1|1} = \left(A^{(v)}_{i,1}, B^{(v)}_{i,1|0}, B^{(v)}_{i,1|1} \right)',$$

where:

- $A^{(v)}_{i,1} = (cc, i, j)'$,
- $B^{(v)}_{i,1|0} = \left(0, Z^{(v)}_{i,1|0}, 0, \tilde{S1}^{(v)}_{i,1|0}, 0, \tilde{S2}^{(v)}_{i,1|0} \right)'$,
- $B^{(v)}_{i,1|1} = \left(Z^{(v)}_{i,1|1}, \tilde{S1}^{(v)}_{i,1|1}, \tilde{S2}^{(v)}_{i,1|1}, S1^{(v)}_{i,1|1}, S2^{(v)}_{i,1|1} \right)'$.

In this example the covariates $S1^{(v)}_{i,1}, S2^{(v)}_{i,1}$ are observed only on the current date $i+2$ and the covariates $Z^{(v)}_{i,1}, \tilde{S1}^{(v)}_{i,1}, \tilde{S2}^{(v)}_{i,1}$ are observed on dates $i+1$ and $i+2$. Then it is implicitly assumed a Markov property of order 1 for the processes $(S1^{(v)}_{i,j|k})_{k \in \mathbb{N}_0}$ and $(S2^{(v)}_{i,j|k})_{k \in \mathbb{N}_0}$ and of order 2 for the processes $(Z^{(v)}_{i,j|k})_{k \in \mathbb{N}_0}$, $(\tilde{S1}^{(v)}_{i,j|k})_{k \in \mathbb{N}_0}$ and $(\tilde{S2}^{(v)}_{i,j|k})_{k \in \mathbb{N}_0}$. In this respect it is useful to introduce the following definition. Let $b^{(v)}_{i,j|k}$ be a dynamic variable included in the feature $x^{(v)}_{i,j|k}$. We denote by historical depth of $b^{(v)}_{i,j|k}$ the maximum $\theta \in \{1, \ldots, k\}$ for which $b^{(v)}_{i,j|k-(\theta-1)}$ is included in $x^{(v)}_{i,j|k}$. Generalizing the previous example, we can say that if $b^{(v)}_{i,j|k}$ has historical depth θ, then a Markov property of order θ is implicitly assumed for the process $(b^{(v)}_{i,j|k})_{k \in \mathbb{N}_0}$.

As previously mentioned, in Section 9 we shall consider multiyear predictions. It is important to observe that in this case a dynamic variable can play the role of both an explanatory and a response variable. This is typical in dynamic modeling. For example, in a prediction from t to $t+2$, the variable $\tilde{S1}^{(v)}_{i,j|t-(i+j)+1}$ could be chosen as a component of the frequency response variable $F^{(v)}_{i,j|t-(i+j)+1}$ in the prediction from t to $t+1$ and as a component of the feature $x^{(v)}_{i,j|t-(i+j)+1}$ in the next prediction from $t+1$ to $t+2$.

As is also clearly recognized in Taylor et al. (2008), an important issue in multiperiod prediction concerns the use of the case reserves. The amount of the type-1 and type-2 case reserve $R1^{(v)}_{i,j|k}$ and $R2^{(v)}_{i,j|k}$ should provide useful information for the claim settlement process. A correct use of this information will typically require a joint dynamic modeling of the claim payment and the case reserve processes. A set of additional model assumptions useful to this aim is provided in Section 10.3.

6. Organization of Data for the Estimation

Since the considerations we present in this section apply to both the frequency and the severity model, we use here the more general notation of problem (2), where (x, Y) is used to denote the feature-response pairs. The exposition can be specified for the frequency or the severity model by skipping to the (x, F) or $(\tilde{x}, S)$ notation, respectively.

Since the regression functions in (2) depend on the lag ℓ, in order to make predictions at time I we need the $I-1$ estimates:

$$\hat{\mu}_\ell, \quad \ell = 0, 1, \ldots, I-2.$$

Each of these estimates is based on historical observations, which are given by the relevant pairs feature-response of claims reported at time $t = I$. Precisely, the estimate $\hat{\mu}_\ell$ at time $t = I$, for $\ell = 0, 1, \ldots, I-2$, is based on the set of *lag observations*:

$$\mathcal{D}_\ell := \mathcal{D}^C_\ell \cup \mathcal{D}^P_\ell,$$

where:

$$\mathcal{D}^C_\ell := \left\{ \left(x^{(v)}_{i,j|\ell-j}, Y^{(v)}_{i,j|\ell-j+1} \right);\ 1 \leq i \leq I-\ell-1,\ \underline{j}_i \leq j \leq \ell,\ 1 \leq v \leq N_{i,j} \right\} : \quad \text{calibration set},$$

$$\mathcal{D}^P_\ell := \left\{ \left(x^{(v)}_{I-\ell,j|\ell-j},\ \cdot\ \right);\ \underline{j}_{I-\ell} \leq j \leq \ell,\ 1 \leq v \leq N_{I-\ell,j} \right\} : \quad \text{prediction set},$$

with $\underline{j}_i \geq 0$ the minimum reporting delay observed for accident year i^2. Given the model assumptions the pairs $\left(x^{(v)}_{i,j|\ell-j}, Y^{(v)}_{i,j|\ell-j+1} \right)$ in the calibration set can be considered independent observations of the random variables feature-response for lag ℓ and can be used for the estimation of the corresponding prediction function in the prediction set. Therefore, we calibrate using CARTs the prediction function μ_ℓ on $\mathcal{D}^C_\ell$, where the pairs feature-response are observed, and apply the resulting calibrated function $\hat{\mu}_\ell$ to the features in $\mathcal{D}^P_\ell$ in order to forecast the corresponding, not yet observed, response variables $Y^{(v)}_{I-\ell,j|\ell-j+1}$. These are predicted as:

$$\hat{Y}^{(v)}_{I-\ell,j|\ell-j+1} := \hat{\mathbb{E}} \left[Y^{(v)}_{I-\ell,j|\ell-j+1} \Big| \mathcal{F}_I \right] = \hat{\mu}_\ell \left(x^{(v)}_{I-\ell,j|\ell-j} \right), \quad \underline{j}_{I-\ell} \leq j \leq \ell,\ 1 \leq v \leq N_{I-\ell,j}.$$

In Table 1 the data structure is illustrated for a very simplified portfolio with $I = 4$ accident years, $\underline{j}_i \equiv 0$ and only one claim for each block (i, j), i.e., $N_{i,j} \equiv 1$. Columns refer to calendar years $t = 1, \ldots, 4$. Cells with "·" refer to dates where the claims are not yet occurred. Cells with "no" (*not observed*) refer to dates where the claims are occurred, but their feature is not yet observed because of reporting delay (these features would have $k < 0$). Observations in the last column cannot be used because at date I the responses with $k > I - (i+j)$ are not yet observed. Cells with observations useful for the calibration are highlighted in pink color.

---

² It can happen, for example, that only claims reported from calendar year y onwards are observed, which implies $i + j \geq y$, i.e., $\underline{j}_i = (y - i) \vee 0$.

Table 1. Pairs feature-response observed at time $I = 4$ for a claims portfolio with $N_{i,j} \equiv 1$. In cells with "no" features are not observed because of reporting delay. Responses on the last column are not yet observed.

				Feature-response Pairs at Calendar Years $t = i+j+k$, $t' = t+1$			
cc	ay: i	rd: j	v	$t = 1$	$t = 2$	$t = 3$	$t = 4 = I$
1	1	0	1	$\left(x_{1,0\|0'}^{(1)}, Y_{1,0\|1}^{(1)}\right)$	$\left(x_{1,0\|1'}^{(1)}, Y_{1,0\|2}^{(1)}\right)$	$\left(x_{1,0\|2'}^{(1)}, Y_{1,0\|3}^{(1)}\right)$	$\left(x_{1,0\|3'}^{(1)} \quad \cdot \right)$
2	1	1	1	no	$\left(x_{1,1\|0'}^{(1)}, Y_{1,1\|1}^{(1)}\right)$	$\left(x_{1,1\|1'}^{(1)}, Y_{1,1\|2}^{(1)}\right)$	$\left(x_{1,1\|2'}^{(1)} \quad \cdot \right)$
3	1	2	1	no	no	$\left(x_{1,2\|0'}^{(1)}, Y_{1,2\|1}^{(1)}\right)$	$\left(x_{1,2\|1'}^{(1)} \quad \cdot \right)$
4	1	3	1	no	no	no	$\left(x_{1,3\|0'}^{(1)} \quad \cdot \right)$
5	2	0	1	.	$\left(x_{2,0\|0'}^{(1)}, Y_{2,0\|1}^{(1)}\right)$	$\left(x_{2,0\|1'}^{(1)}, Y_{2,0\|2}^{(1)}\right)$	$\left(x_{2,0\|2'}^{(1)} \quad \cdot \right)$
6	2	1	1	.	no	$\left(x_{2,1\|0'}^{(1)}, Y_{2,1\|1}^{(1)}\right)$	$\left(x_{2,1\|1'}^{(1)} \quad \cdot \right)$
7	2	2	1	.	no	no	$\left(x_{2,2\|0'}^{(1)} \quad \cdot \right)$
8	3	0	1	.	.	$\left(x_{3,0\|0'}^{(1)}, Y_{3,0\|1}^{(1)}\right)$	$\left(x_{3,0\|1'}^{(1)} \quad \cdot \right)$
9	3	1	1	.	.	no	$\left(x_{3,1\|0'}^{(1)} \quad \cdot \right)$
10	4	0	1	.	.	.	$\left(x_{4,0\|0'}^{(1)} \quad \cdot \right)$

A more convenient presentation of data is provided in Table 2 where the observations are organized by lag, i.e., with columns corresponding to lags $\ell = 0, \ldots, I - 1 = 3$. Intuitively, the feature $x_{i,j|k}^{(v)}$ can be thought of as being allocated on the row (i, j, v) of the table from column $j + k$ back to the first column. Data on the last column $\ell = 3$ can be dropped, since responses have never been observed at time I for this lag. Similarly, row 4, corresponding to claims $C_{1,3}^{(v)}$, can also be dropped.

Table 2. Pairs feature-response observed at time $I = 4$ organized by lag. Data on last column and row 4 cannot be used for prediction.

				Feature-response Pairs Reorganized by Lag ($\ell = j + k$)			
cc	ay: i	rd: j	v	$\ell = 0$	$\ell = 1$	$\ell = 2$	$\ell = 3$
1	1	0	1	$\left(x_{1,0\|0'}^{(1)}, Y_{1,0\|1}^{(1)}\right)$	$\left(x_{1,0\|1'}^{(1)}, Y_{1,0\|2}^{(1)}\right)$	$\left(x_{1,0\|2'}^{(1)}, Y_{1,0\|3}^{(1)}\right)$	$\left(x_{1,0\|3'}^{(1)} \quad \cdot \right)$
2	1	1	1	no	$\left(x_{1,1\|0'}^{(1)}, Y_{1,1\|1}^{(1)}\right)$	$\left(x_{1,1\|1'}^{(1)}, Y_{1,1\|2}^{(1)}\right)$	$\left(x_{1,1\|2'}^{(1)} \quad \cdot \right)$
3	1	2	1	no	no	$\left(x_{1,2\|0'}^{(1)}, Y_{1,2\|1}^{(1)}\right)$	$\left(x_{1,2\|1'}^{(1)} \quad \cdot \right)$
4	1	3	1	no	no	no	$\left(x_{1,3\|0'}^{(1)} \quad \cdot \right)$
5	2	0	1	$\left(x_{2,0\|0'}^{(1)}, Y_{2,0\|1}^{(1)}\right)$	$\left(x_{2,0\|1'}^{(1)}, Y_{2,0\|2}^{(1)}\right)$	$\left(x_{2,0\|2'}^{(1)} \quad \cdot \right)$	.
6	2	1	1	no	$\left(x_{2,1\|0'}^{(1)}, Y_{2,1\|1}^{(1)}\right)$	$\left(x_{2,1\|1'}^{(1)} \quad \cdot \right)$	.
7	2	2	1	no	no	$\left(x_{2,2\|0'}^{(1)} \quad \cdot \right)$	.
8	3	0	1	$\left(x_{3,0\|0'}^{(1)}, Y_{3,0\|1}^{(1)}\right)$	$\left(x_{3,0\|1'}^{(1)} \quad \cdot \right)$	(. , .)	.
9	3	1	1	no	$\left(x_{3,1\|0'}^{(1)} \quad \cdot \right)$	(. , .)	.
10	4	0	1	$\left(x_{4,0\|0'}^{(1)} \quad \cdot \right)$	(. , .)	(. , .)	.

We are then led to the representation in Table 3, which shows a "triangular" structure resembling the data structure typically used in classical claims reserving. In this table observations highlighted in pink color in column ℓ (where the response is observed) provide the dataset $\mathcal{D}_\ell^C$ used for the calibration of $\widehat{\mu}_\ell$. For example, for $\ell = 1$ data refers to claims with identification number cc $= 1, 2, 5, 6$. The feature of claims 1 and 2, belonging to accident year 1, is observed up to time $t = i + \ell = 4$, but only features observed up to time $t = 3$ can be used for the estimation. For claims 2, 3, which are reported with a one-year delay, historical data is missing for calendar year 1, 2, respectively. Cells highlighted in green color correspond to the data sets $\mathcal{D}_\ell^P$, $\ell = 0, 1, 2$, used for the estimates $\widehat{Y}_{I-\ell,j|\ell-j+1}^{(v)}$ of the responses, which replace the missing values in Table 2.

Table 3. Pairs feature-response organized by lag relevant for prediction at time $I = 4$. Responses on the "last diagonal" (green cells) are not yet observed and require one-year forecasts, which are denoted by $\widehat{Y}$. In the two remaining "diagonals" neither the responses nor the features are yet observed; two-year and three-year forecasts are required in these cases.

cc	ay: i	rd: j	v	$\ell = 0$	$\ell = 1$	$\ell = 2$
1	1	0	1	$\left(x_{1,0\|0}^{(1)}, Y_{1,0\|1}^{(1)}\right)$	$\left(x_{1,0\|1}^{(1)}, Y_{1,0\|2}^{(1)}\right)$	$\left(x_{1,0\|2}^{(1)}, Y_{1,0\|3}^{(1)}\right)$
2	1	1	1	no	$\left(x_{1,1\|0}^{(1)}, Y_{1,1\|1}^{(1)}\right)$	$\left(x_{1,1\|1}^{(1)}, Y_{1,1\|2}^{(1)}\right)$
3	1	2	1	no	no	$\left(x_{1,2\|0}^{(1)}, Y_{1,2\|1}^{(1)}\right)$
5	2	0	1	$\left(x_{2,0\|0}^{(1)}, Y_{2,0\|1}^{(1)}\right)$	$\left(x_{2,0\|1}^{(1)}, Y_{2,0\|2}^{(1)}\right)$	$\left(x_{2,0\|2}^{(1)}, \widehat{Y}_{2,0\|3}^{(1)}\right)$
6	2	1	1	no	$\left(x_{2,1\|0}^{(1)}, Y_{2,1\|1}^{(1)}\right)$	$\left(x_{2,1\|1}^{(1)}, \widehat{Y}_{2,1\|2}^{(1)}\right)$
7	2	2	1	no	no	$\left(x_{2,2\|0}^{(1)}, \widehat{Y}_{2,2\|1}^{(1)}\right)$
8	3	0	1	$\left(x_{3,0\|0}^{(1)}, Y_{3,0\|1}^{(1)}\right)$	$\left(x_{3,0\|1}^{(1)}, \widehat{Y}_{3,0\|2}^{(1)}\right)$	.
9	3	1	1	no	$\left(x_{3,1\|0}^{(1)}, \widehat{Y}_{3,1\|1}^{(1)}\right)$	.
10	4	0	1	$\left(x_{4,0\|0}^{(1)}, \widehat{Y}_{4,0\|1}^{(1)}\right)$	.	.

7. Using CARTs for Calibration

7.1. Basic Concepts of CART Techniques

As we have seen, the general form of our one-year prediction problems at time I can be given by:

$$\mathbb{E}\left[Y_{I-\ell,j|\ell-j+1}^{(v)} \Big| \mathcal{F}_I\right] = \mu_\ell\left(x_{I-\ell,j|\ell-j}^{(v)}\right), \quad \ell = 0, \ldots, I-2, \tag{11}$$

which will be specified as a frequency or a severity model according to the specific application. For each lag we calibrate the prediction function μ_ℓ in (11) with CART techniques. Classical references for CART methods are the work Breiman et al. (1998) and Section 9.2 in Hastie et al. (2008). In a CART approach to the prediction problem (11) the $\widehat{\mu}_\ell$ function is *piece-wise constant* on a specified partition:

$$\mathcal{P}_\ell := \left\{\mathcal{R}_\ell^{(1)}, \ldots, \mathcal{R}_\ell^{(R_\ell)}\right\}, \tag{12}$$

of the feature space $\mathcal{X}$, where the elements (regions) $\mathcal{R}_\ell^{(r)}$, $r = 1, \ldots, R_\ell$, of $\mathcal{P}_\ell$ are (hyper)rectangles, i.e., for given ℓ there exist R_ℓ constants $\bar{\mu}_\ell^{(r)}$, $r = 1, \ldots, R_\ell$, such that:

$$\widehat{\mu}_\ell\left(x_{I-\ell,j|\ell-j}^{(v)}\right) = \sum_{r=1}^{R_\ell} \bar{\mu}_\ell^{(r)} \mathbf{1}_{\left\{x_{I-\ell,j|\ell-j}^{(v)} \in \mathcal{R}_\ell^{(r)}\right\}}. \tag{13}$$

The peculiarity of CART techniques consists of the method of choice of partition $\mathcal{P}_\ell$. This is determined on the calibration set $\mathcal{D}_\ell^C$ by assigning to the same rectangle observations (x, Y) which are in some sense more similar. The region $\mathcal{R}_\ell^{(r)}$ is the r-th leaf of a binary tree which is grown by successively partitioning $\mathcal{D}_\ell^C$ through the solution of standardized binary split questions (see Section 5.1.2 in Wüthrich and Buser (2019) for definition). According to the method chosen for the recursive splitting, a *loss function*, or *impurity measure*, $\mathcal{L}$ is specified, and at each step, the split which reduces $\mathcal{L}$ most is the one chosen for the next binary split. The rule by which $\hat{\mu}_\ell^{(r)}$ is computed depends on the method chosen. For example, $\hat{\mu}_\ell^{(r)}$ can be the empirical mean of the response variables if these are quantitative or it can be the category with maximal empirical frequency (maximal class) if the responses are categorical.

In a first stage a binary tree is grown with a large size, i.e., many leaves. In a second stage the initial tree is *pruned* using K-fold cross-validation techniques. Using the cross-validation error a *cost-complexity parameter* is computed as a function of the tree size and the optimal size is that corresponding to a cost-complexity value sufficiently low, according to a given criterion (usually we use the one-standard-error rule). The leaves of this optimally pruned tree are the elements $\mathcal{R}_\ell^{(r)}$ of the partition $\mathcal{P}_\ell$ in (12). The expectations in (11) are then estimated by applying the optimal partition $\mathcal{P}_\ell$ to the prediction set $\mathcal{D}_\ell^P$, i.e.,:

$$\widehat{Y}_{I-\ell,j|\ell-j+1}^{(v)} = \widehat{\mathbb{E}}\left[Y_{I-\ell,j|\ell-j+1}^{(v)} \middle| \mathcal{F}_I\right] = \hat{\mu}_\ell\left(x_{I-\ell,j|\ell-j}^{(v)}\right), \quad \ell = 0,\ldots, I-2,$$

where $\hat{\mu}_\ell$ is given by (13). In D'Agostino et al. (2018) regions $\mathcal{R}_\ell^{(r)}$ and partition $\mathcal{P}_\ell$ are also referred to, respectively, as explanatory classes and explanatory structure (for lag ℓ).

In our applications of CARTs, we shall use the rpart routine implemented in R, see e.g., Therneau et al. (2015).

7.2. Applying CARTs in the Frequency Model

In the frequency section of our frequency-severity model the responses are categorical, then we use classification trees for calibration. In rpart this is obtained with the option method='class', which also implies that the Gini index is used as impurity measure. As previously pointed out, since the rpart routine supports only one-dimensional response variables, instead of using the d-dimensional variables F we formulate the classification problem using the one-dimensional variables defined in (8). From (9) we have:

$$\mathbb{P}\left[W_{I-\ell,j|\ell-j+1}^{(v)} = w \middle| \mathcal{F}_I\right] = p_\ell^{(w)}\left(x_{I-\ell,j|\ell-j}^{(v)}\right), \quad w = 0,\ldots, 2^d - 1. \tag{14}$$

Therefore, the calibration of the prediction function for lag ℓ is performed by determining the optimal partition $\mathcal{P}_\ell$ of the calibration set:

$$\mathcal{D}_\ell^C := \left\{\left(x_{i,j|\ell-j}^{(v)}, W_{i,j|\ell-j+1}^{(v)}\right); \ 1 \leq i \leq I-\ell-1, \ \underline{j}_i \leq j \leq \ell, \ 1 \leq v \leq N_{i,j}\right\},$$

where the calibration of the prediction function reduces to the estimation of the probability distribution $\{p_\ell^{(w)}(\cdot); w = 0,\ldots, 2^d - 1\}$ on each leaf $\mathcal{R}_\ell^{(r)}$ of the optimal partition $\mathcal{P}_\ell$. Formally, for each $r = 1,\ldots, R_\ell$, the rpart routine provides the probabilities:

$$\hat{p}_\ell^{(w,r)}\left(x_{i,j|\ell-j}^{(v)}\right) = \mathbb{P}\left[W_{i,j|\ell-j+1}^{(v)} = w \middle| x_{i,j|\ell-j}^{(v)} \in \mathcal{R}_\ell^{(r)}\right], \quad w = 0,\ldots, 2^d - 1, \tag{15}$$

which are estimated as the empirical frequencies on each leaf of the partition $\mathcal{P}_\ell$ of $\mathcal{D}_\ell^C$. The estimates $\widehat{\mathbb{P}}[W_{I-\ell,j|\ell-j+1}^{(v)} = w | \mathcal{F}_I]$ required in (14) are finally obtained by applying $\mathcal{P}_\ell$ to the prediction set $\mathcal{D}_\ell^P$.

7.3. Applying CARTs in the Severity Model

In the severity section the prediction problem takes the form, from (6):

$$\mathbb{E}\left[S_{I-\ell,j|\ell-j+1}^{(v)} \middle| \mathcal{F}_I, (\tilde{S}_{I-\ell,j|\ell-j+1}^{(v)} = 1)\right] = \tilde{\mu}_\ell\left(\tilde{x}_{I-\ell,j|\ell-j}^{(v)}\right), \tag{16}$$

where we use the generic notations S for $S1, S2$, and $\tilde{S}$ for $\tilde{S}1, \tilde{S}2$. Since the severity is a quantitative variable we use regression trees, which are obtained in rpart with the option method='anova'. In this case, the loss function used is the sum of squared errors (SSE). Given the normality assumption (H5) the SSE minimization performed by the binary splitting algorithm provides a log-likelihood minimization in this non-parametric setting.

The important point here is that since (16) is a conditional model, the set of observed feature-response pairs where the prediction function is calibrated must include only claims for which a payment was made at the response date. Therefore, the calibration set is formally specified as:

$$\mathcal{D}_\ell^C := \left\{ \left(\tilde{x}_{i,j|\ell-j'}^{(v)}, S_{i,j|\ell-j+1}^{(v)} \right) \middle| \left(\bar{S}_{i,j|\ell-j+1}^{(v)} = 1 \right); \ 1 \leq i \leq I - \ell - 1, \ \underline{j}_i \leq j \leq \ell, \ 1 \leq v \leq N_{i,j} \right\}.$$

Similarly, the prediction set is given by:

$$\mathcal{D}_\ell^P := \left\{ \left(\tilde{x}_{I-\ell,j|\ell-j'}^{(v)} \quad \cdot \quad \right) \middle| \left(\bar{S}_{I-\ell,j|\ell-j+1}^{(v)} = 1 \right); \ \underline{j}_i \leq j \leq \ell, \ 1 \leq v \leq N_{i,j} \right\}.$$

This corresponds to the fact that the severity calibration, as being a conditional calibration, must be run after the corresponding frequency calibration has been made, and must be performed on the leaves of the frequency model where a claim payment was made at time $i + \ell + 1$. From the function $\widehat{\bar{\mu}}_\ell$ calibrated in this way one obtains:

$$\widehat{\mathbb{E}}\left[S_{I-\ell,j|\ell-j+1}^{(v)} \middle| \mathcal{F}_I, \left(\bar{S}_{I-\ell,j|\ell-j+1}^{(v)} = 1 \right) \right] = \bar{\bar{\mu}}_\ell^{(r)}\left(\tilde{x}_{I-\ell,j|\ell-j}^{(v)} \right), \ \tilde{x}_{I-\ell,j|\ell-j}^{(v)} \in \mathcal{R}_\ell^{(r)}, \ r = 1, \ldots, R_\ell.$$

As in (7) the estimate of the payment-unconditional expectations is then given by:

$$\widehat{S}_{I-\ell,j|\ell-j+1}^{(v)} = \widehat{\mathbb{E}}\left[S_{I-\ell,j|\ell-j+1}^{(v)} \middle| \mathcal{F}_I \right] = \widehat{\bar{\mu}}_\ell\left(\tilde{x}_{I-\ell,j|\ell-j}^{(v)} \right) \widehat{\mathbb{P}}\left[\bar{S}_{I-\ell,j|\ell-j+1}^{(v)} = 1 \middle| \mathcal{F}_I \right].$$

The final probability estimate in this expression is given by the frequency model, provided that the binary variable $\bar{S}_{I-\ell,j|\ell-j+1}^{(v)}$ has been included in the response $W_{I-\ell,j|\ell-j+1}^{(v)}$.

8. Examples of One-Year Predictions in Motor Insurance

In these first examples we consider one-year predictions based on data from the Italian MTPL line at the observation date 2015. As previously mentioned, we denote by S1 NoCARD payments and by S2 CARD payments (for details on CARD and NoCARD regime see D'Agostino et al. 2018). We have:

- Observed accident years: from 2010 to 2015. Then $i = 1, \ldots, I$ with $I = 6$.
- Only claims reported from 2013 onwards are observed, hence for accident year i, one has $j = \underline{j}_i, \ldots, 6 - i$, with $\underline{j}_i = (4 - i) \vee 0$.
- The pairs feature-response are observed for lags $\ell = 0, \ldots, I - 2 = 4$ (5 estimation steps).

The total number of reported claims in this portfolio is $\sum_{i,j} N_{i,j} = 468,108$. The "triangular" structure of the data is illustrated in Table 4, where the number $N_{i,j}$ of claims in each block (i, j) is also reported. In each column, i.e., for each lag, the cells in the calibration set $\mathcal{D}_\ell^C$ are highlighted in pink and those in the prediction set $\mathcal{D}_\ell^P$ in green color. A rather short claim history ("last 3 diagonals") is observed in this portfolio. This data however is interesting because the information on lawyer involved is available, which can be useful to illustrate early-warning applications of claim watching.

Table 4. Pairs feature-response organized by lag relevant for prediction at time $I = 6$ in the considered claims portfolio.

ay: i	rd: j	v	Feature-response at Lag ℓ				
			$\ell = 0$	$\ell = 1$	$\ell = 2$	$\ell = 3$	$\ell = 4$
1	3	$1,\ldots,130$	no	no	no	$\left(x_{1,3\|0'}^{(v)}, F_{1,3\|1}^{(v)}\right)$	$\left(x_{1,3\|1'}^{(v)}, F_{1,3\|2}^{(v)}\right)$
1	4	$1,\ldots,68$	no	no	no	no	$\left(x_{1,4\|0'}^{(v)}, F_{1,4\|1}^{(v)}\right)$
2	2	$1,\ldots,871$	no	no	$\left(x_{2,2\|0'}^{(v)}, F_{2,2\|1}^{(v)}\right)$	$\left(x_{2,2\|1'}^{(v)}, F_{2,2\|2}^{(v)}\right)$	$\left(x_{2,2\|2'}^{(v)}, \cdot\right)$
2	3	$1,\ldots,119$	no	no	no	$\left(x_{2,3\|0'}^{(v)}, F_{2,3\|1}^{(v)}\right)$	$\left(x_{2,3\|1'}^{(v)}, \cdot\right)$
2	4	$1,\ldots,30$	no	no	no	no	$\left(x_{2,4\|0'}^{(v)}, \cdot\right)$
3	1	$1,\ldots,10,778$	no	$\left(x_{3,1\|0'}^{(v)}, F_{3,1\|1}^{(v)}\right)$	$\left(x_{3,1\|1'}^{(v)}, F_{3,1\|2}^{(v)}\right)$	$\left(x_{3,1\|2'}^{(v)}, \cdot\right)$	$\cdot$
3	2	$1,\ldots,623$	no	no	$\left(x_{3,2\|0'}^{(v)}, F_{3,2\|1}^{(v)}\right)$	$\left(x_{3,2\|1'}^{(v)}, \cdot\right)$	$\cdot$
3	3	$1,\ldots,97$	no	no	no	$\left(x_{3,3\|0'}^{(v)}, \cdot\right)$	$\cdot$
4	0	$1,\ldots,144,820$	$\left(x_{4,0\|0'}^{(v)}, F_{4,0\|1}^{(v)}\right)$	$\left(x_{4,0\|1'}^{(v)}, F_{4,0\|2}^{(v)}\right)$	$\left(x_{4,0\|2'}^{(v)}, \cdot\right)$	$\cdot$	$\cdot$
4	1	$1,\ldots,10,767$	no	$\left(x_{4,1\|0'}^{(v)}, F_{4,1\|1}^{(v)}\right)$	$\left(x_{4,1\|1'}^{(v)}, \cdot\right)$	$\cdot$	$\cdot$
4	2	$1,\ldots,519$	no	no	$\left(x_{4,2\|0'}^{(v)}, \cdot\right)$	$\cdot$	$\cdot$
5	0	$1,\ldots,140,256$	$\left(x_{5,0\|0'}^{(v)}, F_{5,0\|1}^{(v)}\right)$	$\left(x_{5,0\|1'}^{(v)}, \cdot\right)$	$\cdot$	$\cdot$	$\cdot$
5	1	$1,\ldots,10,112$	no	$\left(x_{5,1\|0'}^{(v)}, \cdot\right)$	$\cdot$	$\cdot$	$\cdot$
6	0	$1,\ldots,148,918$	$\left(x_{6,0\|0'}^{(v)}, \cdot\right)$	$\cdot$	$\cdot$	$\cdot$	$\cdot$

8.1. Prediction of Events Using the Frequency Model

In this section, we consider the prediction problem of event occurrences in the next year $I + 1$ and, for illustration, we present a frequency model for the lag $\ell = 1$, thus considering for prediction only the claims of accident year $I - 1 = 5$, i.e., the claims $C_{5,j}^{(v)}$, $j = 0, 1$, $v = 1, \ldots, N_{5,j}$. In our data $N_{5,0} = 140,256$ and $N_{5,1} = 10,112$, therefore $\left|\mathcal{D}_1^P\right| = 150,368$. The observations in the calibration set are $\left|\mathcal{D}_1^C\right| = N_{3,1} + N_{4,0} + N_{4,1} = 166,365$. Let us suppose we want to make prediction of the following indicators at time $I + 1 = 7$, $j = 0, 1$:

$$\tilde{S1}_{5,j|2-j}^{(v)} = \mathbf{1}_{\left\{C_{5,j}^{(v)} \text{ has a type-1 payment at time } 7\right\}},$$

$$\tilde{S2}_{5,j|2-j}^{(v)} = \mathbf{1}_{\left\{C_{5,j}^{(v)} \text{ has a type-2 payment at time } 7\right\}},$$

$$Z_{5,j|2-j}^{(v)} = \mathbf{1}_{\left\{C_{5,j}^{(v)} \text{ is closed at time } 7\right\}},$$

$$L_{5,j|2-j}^{(v)} = \mathbf{1}_{\left\{C_{5,j}^{(v)} \text{ will involve a lawyer at time } 7\right\}}.$$

This choice produces the 4-dimensional response:

$$F_{5,j|2-j}^{(v)} = \left(\tilde{S1}_{5,j|2-j}^{(v)}, \tilde{S2}_{5,j|2-j}^{(v)}, Z_{5,j|2-j}^{(v)}, L_{5,j|2-j}^{(v)}\right)'.$$

We work however with the variable:

$$W_{5,j|2-j}^{(v)} = \tilde{S1}_{5,j|2-j}^{(v)} + 2\,\tilde{S2}_{5,j|2-j}^{(v)} + 4\,Z_{5,j|2-j}^{(v)} + 8\,L_{5,j|2-j}^{(v)},$$

which is a scalar with the 16 possible values $0, \ldots, 15$. These values correspond to 16 "states" of the response, as illustrated in Table 5.

Table 5. Structure of the response variables $W^{(v)}_{I-1,j|2-j}$.

S1	S2	Z	L	W	State of the Response
0	0	0	0	0	ONNO: open without payments and without lawyer
1	0	0	0	1	OYNO: open with S1 payment and without lawyer
0	1	0	0	2	ONYO: open with S2 payment and without lawyer
1	1	0	0	3	OYYO: open with S1 and S2 payment and without lawyer
0	0	1	0	4	CNNO: closed without payments and without lawyer
1	0	1	0	5	CYNO: closed with S1 payment and without lawyer
0	1	1	0	6	CNYO: closed with S2 payment and without lawyer
1	1	1	0	7	CYYO: closed with S1 and S2 payment and without lawyer
0	0	0	1	8	ONNL: open without payments and with lawyer
1	0	0	1	9	OYNL: open with S1 payment and with lawyer
0	1	0	1	10	ONYL: open with S2 payment and with lawyer
1	1	0	1	11	OYYL: open with S1 and S2 payment and with lawyer
0	0	1	1	12	CNNL: closed without payments and with lawyer
1	0	1	1	13	CYNL: closed with S1 payment and with lawyer
0	1	1	1	14	CNYL: closed with S2 payment and with lawyer
1	1	1	1	15	CYYL: closed with S1 and S2 payment and with lawyer

For the feature components of $x^{(v)}_{i,j|2-j}$, $i = 1, \ldots, 5$, $j = 0, 1$, we choose the following variables:

$$\tilde{S1}^{(v)}_{i,j|1-j} = \mathbf{1}_{\left\{ C^{(v)}_{i,j} \text{ has a type-1 payment at time } i+1 \right\}},$$

$$\tilde{S2}^{(v)}_{i,j|1-j} = \mathbf{1}_{\left\{ C^{(v)}_{i,j} \text{ has a type-2 payment at time } i+1 \right\}},$$

$$\tilde{Z}^{(v)}_{i,j|1-j} = \mathbf{1}_{\left\{ C^{(v)}_{i,j} \text{ is closed at time } i+1 \right\}},$$

$$\tilde{L}^{(v)}_{i,j|1-j} = \mathbf{1}_{\left\{ C^{(v)}_{i,j} \text{ involves a lawyer at time } i+1 \right\}},$$

$$\tilde{R1}^{(v)}_{i,j|1-j} = \mathbf{1}_{\left\{ C^{(v)}_{i,j} \text{ has a type-1 case reserve at time } i+1 \right\}},$$

$$\tilde{R2}^{(v)}_{i,j|1-j} = \mathbf{1}_{\left\{ C^{(v)}_{i,j} \text{ has a type-2 case reserve at time } i+1 \right\}}.$$

All these variables are of 0-1 type; however, frequency features need not be of this kind. For example also the case reserve amounts $R1^{(v)}_{i,j|1-j}$ and $R2^{(v)}_{i,j|1-j}$ could be considered.

With this choice for the response variable and the feature components the prediction problem (14) takes the form:

$$\mathbb{P}\left[W^{(v)}_{5,j|2-j} = w\right] = p^{(w)}_1\left(x^{(v)}_{5,j|1-j}\right) \geq 0, \quad w = 0, \ldots, 15,$$

where the probability function $p^{(w)}_1 : \mathcal{X} \mapsto [0,1]^{16}$ is estimated on $\mathcal{D}^C_1$.

As already mentioned, we estimate the probability function $p^{(w)}_1$ under side constraint $\sum_{w=0}^{15} p^{(w)}_1 = 1$ using the routine rpart implemented in R. The input data in $\mathcal{D}^C_1$ is organized as a table (a data frame) where each row corresponds to a claim and in each column the value of the response and of all the feature components observed at different historical dates is reported.

The following R command is used for the calibration, see Therneau et al. (2015) for details[3]:

```
freqtree1 <- rpart(W ~ rd + Z_0 + Z_1 + L_0 + L_1 + P1_0 + P1_1 + P2_0 + P2_1 +
                   T1_0 + T1_1 + T2_0 + T2_1, data=dt_freq1,
                   method='class', control=rpart.control(cp=0.01))
```

where dt_freq1 is the calibration set $\mathcal{D}_1^C$, and the variables are relabeled as follows:

$$W_{i,j|2-j}^{(v)} = \text{W}, \quad Z_{i,j|1-j}^{(v)} = \text{Z\_1}, \quad L_{i,j|1-j}^{(v)} = \text{L\_1}, \quad \tilde{S1}_{i,j|1-j}^{(v)} = \text{P1\_1}, \quad \tilde{S2}_{i,j|1-j}^{(v)} = \text{P2\_1},$$

$$\tilde{R1}_{i,j|1-j}^{(v)} = \text{T1\_1}, \quad \tilde{R2}_{i,j|1-j}^{(v)} = \text{T2\_1}, \quad \underline{j}_i \leq j \leq 1,$$

and:

$$Z_{i,0|0}^{(v)} = \text{Z\_0}, \quad L_{i,0|0}^{(v)} = \text{L\_0}, \quad \tilde{S1}_{i,0|0}^{(v)} = \text{P1\_0}, \quad \tilde{S2}_{i,0|0}^{(v)} = \text{P2\_0}, \quad \tilde{R1}_{i,0|0}^{(v)} = \text{T1\_0}, \quad \tilde{R2}_{i,0|0}^{(v)} = \text{T2\_0}.$$

The rationale of this labelling is that variables with subscript _h, $h = 0, \ldots, \ell$, are observed at time $i+h$ i.e., have historical depth $\theta = \ell - h + 1$. Therefore for $\ell = 1$ variables with _1 have $\theta = 1$ and variables with _0 have $\theta = 2$.

With the previous command a large binary tree, freqtree1, was grown by rpart. In a second step freqtree1 has been pruned using 10-fold cross-validation and applying the one-standard-error rule. The resulting pruned tree is reported in Figure 1, which is obtained by the package rpart.plot.

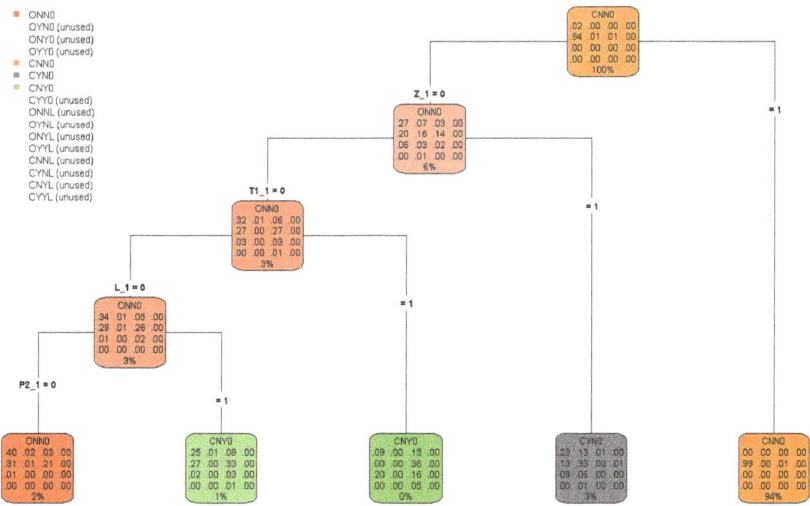

Figure 1. Frequency model: pruned classification tree for lag $\ell = 1$.

The tree has $R_1 = 5$ leaves. In the "palette" associated with each node of the tree the corresponding frequency distribution of the response variable W observed in the calibration set $\mathcal{D}_1^C$ is reported. Therefore the palettes associated with the leaves provide the probability estimates $\hat{p}_1^{(w,r)}$ associated with

---

[3] The value 0.01 of the complexity parameter cp used in this example is rather high. It has been used here to simplify the illustration, since the pruned tree finally obtained with this choice is not too much large. For this reason, this pruned tree is slightly suboptimal. Using a more appropriate value of cp, however, does not change substantially the results that are discussed here.

the regions $\mathcal{R}_1^{(r)}$, $r = 1, \ldots, 5$, of the optimal partition $\mathcal{P}_1$, as shown by expression (15). Frequencies in the palettes are expressed in percent and are rounded to the nearest whole number. The rpart numerical output provides more precise figures.

To illustrate Figure 1 we order the leaves in sequence from left to right, so that the r-th leaf from the left corresponds to the region $\mathcal{R}_1^{(r)}$ of $\mathcal{P}_1$. Let us consider, for example, the claims in the fifth leaf $\mathcal{R}_1^{(5)}$, which have Z_1 = 1. These are the claims in the calibration set that were closed at time 4 and 5 (then with $Z_{i,j|1-j}^{(v)} = 1$, $i = 3, 4$); these claims are the 94% of all claims in the calibration set. Since, under model assumptions, the observed frequencies provide the estimate of the corresponding probabilities at the current time I for event occurrences at time $I + 1$, one can observe that for claims closed at time I there is (about) a 99% probability that they will be closed without payments at time $I + 1$, while there is (about) a 1% probability that they will reopened with a payment. Leaf 4 in the tree contains the claims with Z_1 = 0 and T1_1 = 1. These are the claims in the calibration set (3% of the total) which were open with a type-1 reserve placed on at time 4 and 5, i.e., $(Z_{i,j|1-j}^{(v)} = 0) \cap (\tilde{R1}_{i,j|1-j}^{(v)} = 1)$, $i = 3, 4$. From the frequency table reported in the palette, we conclude that for the claims open with type-1 reserve at time I the most probable state at time $I + 1$ (33% probability) is CYNO, i.e., the state with a type-1 payment and claim closing ($W_{5,j|2-j}^{(v)} = 5$). In leaf 3 we find the claims in the calibration set which at time 4 and 5 were open without type-1 reserve and with a lawyer involved, i.e., $(Z_{i,j|1-j}^{(v)} = 0) \cap (\tilde{R1}_{i,j|1-j}^{(v)} = 0) \cap (L_{i,j|1-j}^{(v)} = 1)$, $i = 3, 4$. These claims are 0.2% of the total. From the frequency table we conclude that for claims that at time I have the same feature the most probable state at time $I + 1$ (36% probability) is CNYO, i.e., the state with a type-2 payment and claim closing ($W_{5,j|2-j}^{(v)} = 6$). In the fourth binary split, which produces the first two leaves in the tree, the splitting criterion is the existence of a type-2 payment (indicator P2_1) for claims which at time 4 and 5 were open without type-1 reserve and without a lawyer. From the frequency tables in the second and the first leaf (referring to about 1% and 2% of the claims of the calibration set, respectively), one finds that if at time I the claim has a type-2 payment, the most probable state at time $I + 1$ (33%) is CNYO; otherwise the most probable state (40%) is ONNO, i.e., it remains open without payments and without involving a lawyer.

It is interesting to note that although we included in the model also explanatory variables observed with historical depth $\theta = 2$ (i.e., feature variables with subscript _0), none of these variables has been considered useful for prediction by the algorithm (after pruning). Only explanatory variables with $\theta = 1$ (subscript _1) has been used for the splits in the pruned tree.

8.2. Possible Use for Early Warnings

For a given claim with $\ell = 1$ let us consider questions as those of type (b) presented in Section 2 (with $\tau = 1$). Formally, for a given claim $C_{5,j}^{(v)}$ in $\mathcal{D}_1^P$ let us consider the event $\left\{ C_{5,j}^{(v)} \text{ will involve a lawyer at time } 7 \right\}$, with indicator $L_{5,j|2-j}^{(v)}$. This corresponds to the events $W_{5,j|2-j}^{(v)} \in \{8, \ldots, 15\}$ hence:

$$\mathbb{P}\left[L_{5,j|2-j}^{(v)} = 1 \right] = \sum_{w=8}^{15} \mathbb{P}\left[W_{5,j|2-j}^{(v)} = w \right].$$

This probability is different in different leaves of the classification tree, then we write:

$$\lambda^{(r)} := \widehat{\mathbb{P}}\left[L_{5,j|2-j}^{(v)} = 1 \Big| C_{5,j}^{(v)} \in \mathcal{R}_1^{(r)} \right] = \sum_{w=8}^{15} \widehat{p}_1^{(w,r)}, \quad r = 1, \ldots R_1.$$

If $n^{(r)}$ denotes the number of claims $C_{5,j}^{(v)}$ belonging to leaf r, the expected number of claims with lag 1 that will involve a lawyer in the next year is given by $\Lambda := \sum_{r=1}^{R_1} \lambda^{(r)} n^{(r)}$.

The values of $\lambda^{(r)}$ and $n^{(r)}$ are reported in Table 6, where the leaves are ordered by decreasing value of the probability $\lambda^{(r)}$. It results that the expected number is $\Lambda = 920$. Since $|\mathcal{D}_1^P| = \sum_{r=1}^{5} n^{(r)} =$

150, 368, only 0.6% of the claims in $\mathcal{D}_1^P$ is expected to involve a lawyer in one year. This data could also be useful for providing information to an early-warning system. For example, a list could be provided of the first 323 claims in the table, i.e., the claims in $\mathcal{D}_1^P$ for which $\lambda^{(r)} > 40\%$.

Table 6. Expectations of involving a lawyer in different leaves.

r	$\lambda^{(r)}$	$n^{(r)}$
3	40.50%	323
4	16.46%	3204
2	5.89%	1495
1	1.63%	1878
5	0.10%	143,468

In Section 11.2 we will present a backtesting exercise for this kind of predictions.

8.3. Prediction of Claim Payments Using the Conditional Severity Model

Once the optimal classification tree in Figure 1 has been obtained for the frequency, for each leaf in this tree two regression functions must be calibrated for the severity, one for type-1 and one for type-2 payments. For the sake of brevity, we illustrate two cases:

1. The estimate of a type-1 (i.e., NoCARD) payment for open claims with type-1 reserve placed on, for which we consider the claims in leaf 4 in the frequency tree in Figure 1.
2. The estimate of a type-2 (i.e., CARD) payment for open claims without type-1 reserve placed on and with lawyer involved, for which we consider the claims in leaf 3 in Figure 1.

Case 1. As pointed out in Section 7.3, since the severity model is a conditional model, for the calibration of the regression function $\tilde{\mu}_\ell^{(1)}$ only the claims for which a type-1 payment is made at the response date are considered. Hence the calibration set for this regression estimate is the subset of claims in leaf 4 of the frequency tree for which a type-1 payment was observed in the response. It results in this calibration set consisting of 2564 claims. For the calibration of this regression tree the following R command is used:

```
sevtree4 <- rpart( S1_2 ~ rd + L_0 + L_1 + S1_0 + S1_1 + S2_0 + S2_1 +
                  R1_0 + R1_1 + R2_0 + R2_1, data=dt_sev4,
                  method='anova', control=rpart.control(cp=0.001))
```

where dt_sev4 is the calibration set and the relabeling is used:

$$S1_{i,j|2-j}^{(v)} = S1\_2, \quad L_{i,j|1-j}^{(v)} = L\_1, \quad S1_{i,j|1-j}^{(v)} = S1\_1, \quad S2_{i,j|1-j}^{(v)} = S2\_1,$$

$$R1_{i,j|1-j}^{(v)} = R1\_1, \quad R2_{i,j|1-j}^{(v)} = R2\_1, \quad j_i \le j \le 1;$$

$$L_{i,0|0}^{(v)} = L\_0, \quad S1_{i,0|0}^{(v)} = S1\_0, \quad S2_{i,0|0}^{(v)} = S2\_0, \quad R1_{i,0|0}^{(v)} = R1\_0, \quad R2_{i,0|0}^{(v)} = R2\_0.$$

As for the frequency case, after the large binary tree sevtree4 was grown by rpart, this was pruned using 10-fold cross-validation and applying the one-standard-error rule. The pruned tree thus obtained is illustrated in Figure 2, provided by rpart.plot.

The feature variable and its critical value used for the binary split are indicated on each node. On the palette attached to the node the empirical mean of payments and the percentage number of observations is reported. The partition provided by the pruned tree consists of 7 leaves. Under model assumptions, the average payment reported in the palette provides the expected value at time $I = 6$ of the type-1 payment at time $I + 1 = 7$.

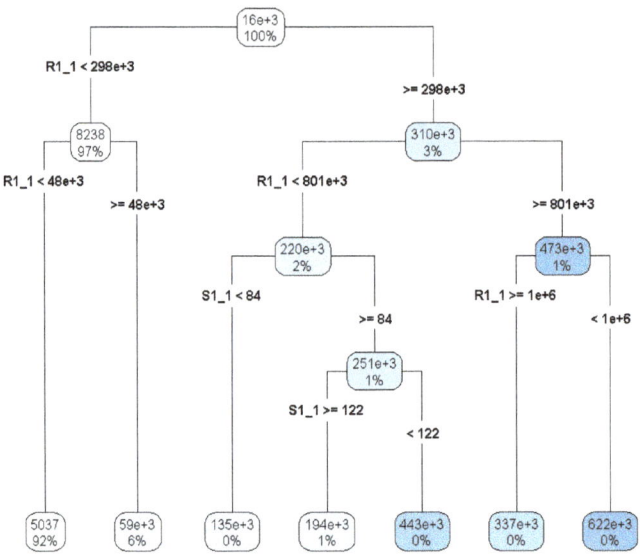

Figure 2. Severity model: pruned regression tree for claims in leaf 4 of the frequency tree.

Case 2. In this case, the calibration set for the severity tree is the subset of claims in leaf 3 of the frequency tree for which a type-2 payment was observed in the response. This calibration set consists of 281 claims. The R command used for this regression tree is similar to that for Case 1. The tree pruned with the usual method is reported in Figure 3.

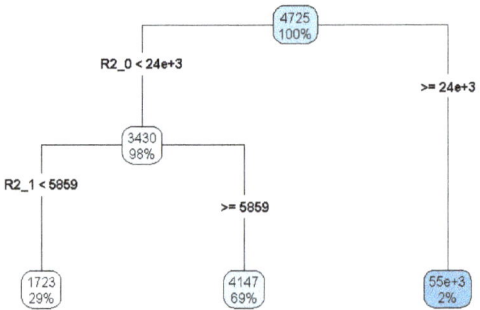

Figure 3. Severity model: pruned regression tree for claims in leaf 3 of the frequency tree.

The partition provided by this tree consists now of 3 leaves. The average payment reported in the palette of each leaf provides the expected value at time 6 of the type-2 payment at time 7 for these claims.

Part II. Multiperiod Predictions and Backtesting

9. Multiperiod Predictions

9.1. The Shift-Forward Procedure and the Self-Sustaining Property

The basic idea underlying the extension of a one-period prediction to a multiperiod prediction in the frequency model can be illustrated as follows. At time $i + j + k = I$, let us consider the claims referring to two contiguous prediction sets $\mathcal{D}_\ell^P, \mathcal{D}_{\ell'}^P$ with $\ell' = \ell + 1$, $\ell = 0, \ldots, I - 3$, that is the claims classes:

$$\mathcal{H} = \left(\mathcal{C}_{i,j}^{(v)} : i = I - \ell, \underline{j}_{I-\ell} \leq j \leq \ell, 1 \leq v \leq N_{I-\ell,j} \right),$$

$$\mathcal{H}' = \left(\mathcal{C}_{i,j}^{(v')} : i = I - \ell', \underline{j}_{I-\ell'} \leq j \leq \ell', 1 \leq v' \leq N_{I-\ell',j} \right).$$

For these two classes the corresponding one-year prediction problem in the frequency model is given by:

$$\mathbb{E}\left[F_{I-\ell,j|\ell-j+1}^{(v)} \Big| \mathcal{F}_I \right] = p_\ell^{(f)} \left(x_{I-\ell,j|\ell-j}^{(v)} \right),$$

$$\mathbb{E}\left[F_{I-\ell',j|\ell'-j+1}^{(v')} \Big| \mathcal{F}_I \right] = p_{\ell'}^{(f)} \left(x_{I-\ell',j|\ell'-j}^{(v')} \right).$$

Assume that the prediction functions of the two problems have been calibrated on the sets $\mathcal{D}_\ell^C$ and $\mathcal{D}_{\ell'}^C$, respectively, with the resulting estimates for time $I + 1$:

$$\widehat{F}_{I-\ell,j|\ell-j+1}^{(v)} = \widehat{p}_\ell^{(f)} \left(x_{I-\ell,j|\ell-j}^{(v)} \right),$$

$$\widehat{F}_{I-\ell',j|\ell'-j+1}^{(v')} = \widehat{p}_{\ell'}^{(f)} \left(x_{I-\ell',j|\ell'-j}^{(v')} \right).$$

Our aim is to derive an estimate of the two-year response $F_{I-\ell,j|\ell-j+2}^{(v)}$ for the claims $\mathcal{C}_{i,j}^{(v)}$ in class $\mathcal{H}$, i.e., with accident year $I - \ell$.

Assume that the feature and the response for claims in class $\mathcal{H}$ are specified so that:

$$\widehat{F}_{I-\ell,j|\ell-j+1}^{(v)} \supseteq \widehat{B}_{I-\ell,j|\ell-j+1}^{(v)}, \qquad (17)$$

i.e., the estimated response variable for claims in class $\mathcal{H}$ contains an estimate of the next year dynamic component of the feature $x_{I-\ell,j|\ell-j+1}^{(v)}$ of these claims, see expression (10). Following D'Agostino et al. (2018) a property such as (17) is referred to as *self-sustaining property*. Then we can estimate the response at time $I + 2$ as:

$$\widehat{F}_{I-\ell,j|\ell-j+2}^{(v)} = \widehat{p}_{\ell+1}^{(f)} \left(\widehat{x}_{I-\ell,j|\ell-j+1}^{(v)} \right),$$

where $\widehat{x}_{i,j|I-i-j+1}^{(v)} = \left(x_{i,j|I-i-j'}^{(v)} \widehat{B}_{i,j|I-i-j+1}^{(v)} \right)'$ is the one-year updated feature of $\mathcal{C}_{i,j}^{(v)} \in \mathcal{H}$. In this procedure the two-year response estimate for claims in class $\mathcal{H}$ (whose one-year response has been estimated using the $\widehat{\mu}_\ell$ prediction function) is obtained by the $\widehat{\mu}_{\ell'}$ prediction function, which has been estimated for claims in class $\mathcal{H}'$ but is now applied to the claim feature updated using $\widehat{\mu}_\ell$.

The previous shift-forward procedure applied for all lags $\ell = 0, \ldots, I - 3$ provides all the two-year predictions, i.e., the entire "second new diagonal" of estimates in the "data triangle", provided that property (17) holds for each lag.

As an example, let us consider in Table 7 the time I estimates for claims of accident year $I = 6$ (class $\mathcal{H}$) and of accident year $I - 1 = 5$ (class $\mathcal{H}'$), with corresponding lags $\ell = 0$ and $\ell' = 1$. We have the problems:

$$\mathbb{E}\left[F^{(v)}_{6,0|1}\Big|\mathcal{F}_6\right] = \widehat{p}^{(f)}_0\left(x^{(v)}_{6,0|0}\right), \quad \mathbb{E}\left[F^{(v)}_{5,0/1|1/0+1}\Big|\mathcal{F}_6\right] = \widehat{p}^{(f)}_1\left(x^{(v)}_{5,0/1|1/0}\right),$$

which, after calibration at time 6 on $\mathcal{D}^{\mathcal{C}}_0$ and $\mathcal{D}^{\mathcal{C}}_1$, respectively, provide the estimates for time 7:

$$\widehat{F}^{(v)}_{6,0|1} = \widehat{p}^{(f)}_0\left(x^{(v)}_{6,0|0}\right), \quad \widehat{F}^{(v)}_{5,0/1|1/0+1} = \widehat{p}^{(f)}_1\left(x^{(v)}_{5,0/1|1/0}\right).$$

Table 7. Creating "future diagonals" by multiyear predictions.

ay: i	rd: j	v	$\ell = 0$	$\ell = 1$	$\ell = 2$	$\ell = 3$	$\ell = 4$
1	3	$1,\ldots,N_{1,3}$	no	no	no	$\left(x^{(v)}_{1,3\|0},F^{(v)}_{1,3\|1}\right)$	$\left(x^{(v)}_{1,3\|1},F^{(v)}_{1,3\|2}\right)$
1	4	$1,\ldots,N_{1,4}$	no	no	no	no	$\left(x^{(v)}_{1,4\|0},F^{(v)}_{1,4\|1}\right)$
2	2	$1,\ldots,N_{2,2}$	no	no	$\left(x^{(v)}_{2,2\|0},F^{(v)}_{2,2\|1}\right)$	$\left(x^{(v)}_{2,2\|1},F^{(v)}_{2,2\|2}\right)$	$\left(x^{(v)}_{2,2\|2},\widehat{F}^{(v)}_{2,2\|3}\right)$
2	3	$1,\ldots,N_{2,3}$	no	no	no	$\left(x^{(v)}_{2,3\|0},F^{(v)}_{2,3\|1}\right)$	$\left(x^{(v)}_{2,3\|1},\widehat{F}^{(v)}_{2,3\|2}\right)$
2	4	$1,\ldots,N_{2,4}$	no	no	no	no	$\left(x^{(v)}_{2,4\|0},\widehat{F}^{(v)}_{2,4\|1}\right)$
3	1	$1,\ldots,N_{3,1}$	no	$\left(x^{(v)}_{3,1\|0},F^{(v)}_{3,1\|1}\right)$	$\left(x^{(v)}_{3,1\|1},F^{(v)}_{3,1\|2}\right)$	$\left(x^{(v)}_{3,1\|2},\widehat{F}^{(v)}_{3,1\|3}\right)$	$\left(\widehat{x}^{(v)}_{3,1\|3},\widehat{F}^{(v)}_{3,1\|4}\right)$
3	2	$1,\ldots,N_{3,2}$	no	no	$\left(x^{(v)}_{3,2\|0},F^{(v)}_{3,2\|1}\right)$	$\left(x^{(v)}_{3,2\|1},\widehat{F}^{(v)}_{3,2\|2}\right)$	$\left(\widehat{x}^{(v)}_{3,2\|2},\widehat{F}^{(v)}_{3,2\|3}\right)$
3	3	$1,\ldots,N_{3,3}$	no	no	no	$\left(x^{(v)}_{3,3\|0},\widehat{F}^{(v)}_{3,3\|1}\right)$	$\left(\widehat{x}^{(v)}_{3,3\|1},\widehat{F}^{(v)}_{3,3\|2}\right)$
4	0	$1,\ldots,N_{4,0}$	$\left(x^{(v)}_{4,0\|0},F^{(v)}_{4,0\|1}\right)$	$\left(x^{(v)}_{4,0\|1},F^{(v)}_{4,0\|2}\right)$	$\left(x^{(v)}_{4,0\|2},\widehat{F}^{(v)}_{4,0\|3}\right)$	$\left(\widehat{x}^{(v)}_{4,0\|3},\widehat{F}^{(v)}_{4,0\|4}\right)$	.
4	1	$1,\ldots,N_{4,1}$	no	$\left(x^{(v)}_{4,1\|0},F^{(v)}_{4,1\|1}\right)$	$\left(x^{(v)}_{4,1\|1},\widehat{F}^{(v)}_{4,1\|2}\right)$	$\left(\widehat{x}^{(v)}_{4,1\|2},\widehat{F}^{(v)}_{4,1\|3}\right)$	.
4	2	$1,\ldots,N_{4,2}$	no	no	$\left(x^{(v)}_{4,2\|0},\widehat{F}^{(v)}_{4,2\|1}\right)$	$\left(\widehat{x}^{(v)}_{4,2\|1},\widehat{F}^{(v)}_{4,2\|2}\right)$	.
5	0	$1,\ldots,N_{5,0}$	$\left(x^{(v)}_{5,0\|0},F^{(v)}_{5,0\|1}\right)$	$\left(x^{(v)}_{5,0\|1},\widehat{F}^{(v)}_{5,0\|2}\right)$	$\left(\widehat{x}^{(v)}_{5,0\|2},\widehat{F}^{(v)}_{5,0\|3}\right)$	.	.
5	1	$1,\ldots,N_{5,1}$	no	$\left(x^{(v)}_{5,1\|0},\widehat{F}^{(v)}_{5,1\|1}\right)$	$\left(\widehat{x}^{(v)}_{5,1\|1},\widehat{F}^{(v)}_{5,1\|2}\right)$	.	.
6	0	$1,\ldots,N_{6,0}$	$\left(x^{(v)}_{6,0\|0},\widehat{F}^{(v)}_{6,0\|1}\right)$	$\left(\widehat{x}^{(v)}_{6,0\|1},\widehat{F}^{(v)}_{6,0\|2}\right)$	$\left(\widehat{x}^{(v)}_{6,0\|2},\widehat{F}^{(v)}_{6,0\|3}\right)$	.	.

We want to derive an estimate of the two-year response $F^{(v)}_{6,0|2}$ for the claims with accident year 6. If $\widehat{F}^{(v)}_{6,0|1} \supseteq \widehat{B}^{(v)}_{6,0|1}$, i.e., if the one-year response variable for claims of accident year 6 includes an estimate of the next-year updating component of the features $x^{(v)}_{6,0|0}$, then we can estimate the response at time 8 as:

$$\widehat{F}^{(v)}_{6,0|2} = \widehat{p}^{(f)}_1\left(\widehat{x}^{(v)}_{6,0|1}\right),$$

where $\widehat{x}^{(v)}_{6,0|1} = \left(x^{(v)}_{6,0|0},\widehat{B}^{(v)}_{6,0|1}\right)'$. This shift-forward procedure allowed by the self-sustaining property is represented in Table 7 by the first red arrow on the bottom. The same procedure applied for all lags $\ell = 0,\ldots,I-3$ provides the entire "second new diagonal" of estimates i.e., the cells in light blue color in Table 7.

To derive the third new diagonal of estimates, i.e., the three-year predictions for lags $\ell = 0,\ldots,I-3$, we can repeat the previous procedure, provided that the self-sustaining properties hold:

$$\widehat{F}^{(v)}_{I-\ell,j|\ell-j+2} \supseteq \widehat{B}^{(v)}_{I-\ell,j|\ell-j+2}, \quad \ell = 0,\ldots,I-3.$$

In the example of Table 7 the second shift-forward procedure providing the lowest element of the second new diagonal (darker blue cells) is represented by a blue arrow.

24

In general, for the h-th new diagonal, the required properties are:

$$\widehat{F}^{(v)}_{I-\ell,j|\ell-j+h} \supseteq \widehat{B}^{(v)}_{I-\ell,j|\ell-j+h}, \quad h = 1,\ldots,I-1, \quad \ell = 0,\ldots,I-1-h.$$

It should be noted that in all these multiyear prediction procedures only the calibrations for lags $\ell = 0,\ldots,I-3$ made at time I are used.

9.2. Illustration in Terms of Partitions

The multiperiod prediction can be also illustrated in terms of partitions of $\mathcal{X}$. We refer here to the one-dimensional formulation of the frequency response. Following D'Agostino et al. (2018), in terms of the partition elements provided by the classification trees, the self-sustaining property requires that:

For $i = 1,\ldots,I$, $j = 0,\ldots,J$, $v = 1,\ldots,N_{i,j}$, $k \in \mathbb{N}_0$, the response $W^{(v)}_{i,j|k+1}$ and the features $x_{i,j|k}$, $x_{i,j|k+1}$ are such that for $u = 1,\ldots,R_{j+k}$ and $w = 0,1,\ldots,2^d - 1$ it is always possible to calculate the function $\phi_{j+k+1}(u,w)$ defined as:

$$\phi_{j+k+1}(u,w) = r : \left(x^{(v)}_{i,j|k+1} \in \mathcal{R}^{(r)}_{j+k+1}\right) \Big| \left((x^{(v)}_{i,j|k} \in \mathcal{R}^{(u)}_{j+k}) \cap (W^{(v)}_{i,j|k+1} = w)\right), \quad r = 1,\ldots R_{j+k+1}.$$

That is for all i,j,v,k the features $x^{(v)}_{i,j|k}$, $x^{(v)}_{i,j|k+1}$ and the response $W^{(v)}_{i,j|k+1}$ are specified so that any element of the partition $\mathcal{P}_{j+k}$ is mapped by ϕ_{j+k+1} into a unique element of the partition $\mathcal{P}_{j+k+1}$. In principle, this could lead to formulate the multiyear prediction in terms of transition probabilities $\pi_\ell(u,w)$, i.e., the probability of transitioning from one state u of the response $W^{(v)}_{I-\ell,j|\ell-j}$ to one state w of the response $W^{(v)}_{I-\ell,j|\ell-j+1}$.

9.3. Illustration in Terms of Conditional Expectations

As in Wüthrich (2016) the multiperiod prediction can also be expressed in terms of conditional expectations. For the two-year prediction we have:

$$\begin{aligned}
\mathbb{E}\left[F^{(v)}_{I-\ell,j|\ell-j+2}\Big|\mathcal{F}_I\right] &= \mathbb{E}\left[\mathbb{E}\left[F^{(v)}_{I-\ell,j|\ell-j+2}\Big|\mathcal{F}_{I+1}\right]\Big|\mathcal{F}_I\right] \\
&= \mathbb{E}\left[\sum_{f_1,\ldots,f_d} f'\, p^{(f)}_{\ell+1}\left(x^{(v)}_{I-\ell,j|\ell-j+1}\right)\Big|\mathcal{F}_I\right] \\
&= \sum_{f_1,\ldots,f_d} f'\, \mathbb{E}\left[p^{(f)}_{\ell+1}\left(x^{(v)}_{I-\ell,j|\ell-j+1}\right)\Big|\mathcal{F}_I\right] \\
&= \sum_{f_1,\ldots,f_d} f'\, \widehat{p}^{(f)}_{\ell+1}\left(\widehat{x}^{(v)}_{I-\ell,j|\ell-j+1}\right),
\end{aligned}$$

where in the last equality we replaced the probabilities $p^{(f)}_{\ell+1}$ with their $\mathcal{F}_I$-measurable expectations provided by the CART calibration.

10. The Simulation Approach

The analytical calculations involved in both the transition matrix approach and the conditional expectation approach can be very burdensome from a computational point of view. The computational cost depends on the number of dynamic variables to be modeled. For example, with 4 dynamic variables and $I = 10$ the number of possible states of the response W for a claim of accident year I is given by is $4^{2^{I-1}} = 4^{2^9} = 68{,}719{,}476{,}736$. To avoid these difficulties, we take a simulation approach for multiperiod forecasting.

10.1. A Typical Multiperiod Prediction Problem

To illustrate this approach, we consider one of the most important multiperiod prediction problems, which is the basis for individual claims reserving. In the outstanding portfolio, let us consider a specified claim $C_{i,j}^{(v)}$ occurred in accident year i and reported with delay j. The claims portfolio has been observed up to the current date I and we want to predict on this date the total cost (of type 1 and type 2) in the next $\tau \in \mathbb{N}_1$ years. Let us define the cumulated costs:

$$K1_{i,j|I-(i+j)+\tau}^{(v)} = \sum_{h=1}^{\tau} S1_{i,j|I-(i+j)+h}^{(v)}, \quad \tau \in \mathbb{N}_0,$$

$$K2_{i,j|I-(i+j)+\tau}^{(v)} = \sum_{h=1}^{\tau} S2_{i,j|I-(i+j)+h}^{(v)}, \quad \tau \in \mathbb{N}_0,$$

where, obviously, $K1_{i,j|I-(i+j)+0}^{(v)} = K2_{i,j|I-(i+j)+0}^{(v)} = 0$. We can say that $(K1_{i,j|I-(i+j)+\tau}^{(v)})_{\tau \in \mathbb{N}_0}$ and $(K2_{i,j|I-(i+j)+\tau}^{(v)})_{\tau \in \mathbb{N}_0}$ provide the cumulated cost development path, of type 1 and type 2 respectively, of the claim in the future, i.e., on the dates $I+1, I+2, \ldots$. We want to predict these paths, i.e., we want to derive, using prediction trees, the estimates:

$$\widehat{K1}_{i,j|I-(i+j)+\tau}^{(v)} = \widehat{\mathbb{E}}\left[K1_{i,j|I-(i+j)+\tau}^{(v)}\middle|\mathcal{F}_I\right], \quad \tau \in \mathbb{N}_1,$$

$$\widehat{K2}_{i,j|I-(i+j)+\tau}^{(v)} = \widehat{\mathbb{E}}\left[K2_{i,j|I-(i+j)+\tau}^{(v)}\middle|\mathcal{F}_I\right], \quad \tau \in \mathbb{N}_1.$$

In our data we have not observations to make predictions beyond the date $2I - 1$, i.e., for $\tau > I - 1$. If one assumes that the claims are finalized at this date, then we can take the expected cumulated cost at time $2I - 1$ as an estimate of the individual reserve estimate, i.e.:

$$\begin{aligned} E1_{i,j}^{(v)} &= \widehat{K1}_{i,j|2I-(i+j)-1}^{(v)} = \widehat{\mathbb{E}}\left[K1_{i,j|2I-(i+j)-1}^{(v)}\middle|\mathcal{F}_I\right], \\ E2_{i,j}^{(v)} &= \widehat{K2}_{i,j|2I-(i+j)-1}^{(v)} = \widehat{\mathbb{E}}\left[K2_{i,j|2I-(i+j)-1}^{(v)}\middle|\mathcal{F}_I\right], \end{aligned} \quad (18)$$

where $E1_{i,j}^{(v)}$ and $E2_{i,j}^{(v)}$ denote the type-1 and type-2, respectively, reserve estimate at time I of the claim $C_{i,j}^{(v)}$. The total reserve is obviously obtained as $E_{i,j}^{(v)} = E1_{i,j}^{(v)} + E2_{i,j}^{(v)}$.

It is worth noting that if the case reserves are dynamically modeled, one could also obtain the estimates:

$$\begin{aligned} T1_{i,j}^{(v)} &:= \widehat{R1}_{i,j|2I-(i+j)-1}^{(v)} = \widehat{\mathbb{E}}\left[R1_{i,j|2I-(i+j)-1}^{(v)}\middle|\mathcal{F}_I\right], \\ T2_{i,j}^{(v)} &:= \widehat{R2}_{i,j|2I-(i+j)-1}^{(v)} = \widehat{\mathbb{E}}\left[R2_{i,j|2I-(i+j)-1}^{(v)}\middle|\mathcal{F}_I\right]. \end{aligned} \quad (19)$$

If these estimates are different from zero the assumption of claims finalization at time $2I - 1$ can be relaxed and the final case reserve estimates $T1_{i,j}^{(v)}$ and $T2_{i,j}^{(v)}$ can be used as type-1 and type-2, respectively, *tail reserve estimates*. In this case, one obtains comprehensive reserve estimates by adding the tail reserves in (19) to the estimates in (18).

10.2. Simulation of Sample Paths and Reserve Estimates

In the simulation approach the expected cumulated costs of the claim $C_{i,j}^{(v)}$, and as a byproduct the reserve estimates, are obtained by simulating a number N of possible paths of the cost development and then computing the average path, which is obtained as the sample mean of the costs on each date of the paths. We give some details of this procedure. It is convenient to skip again to the "by lag" language in this exposition.

Let us suppose, as usual, that at time I the historical observations on the claims portfolio are sufficient for calibrating the classification tree for the frequency and the regression trees for the conditional severity (of type 1 and 2) for all lags $\ell = 0, \ldots, I-2$. Therefore, at time I all the optimal frequency partitions $\mathcal{P}_\ell$ of the feature space $\mathcal{X}$ and the optimal severity partitions $\mathcal{Q}_\ell^{(1)}, \mathcal{Q}_\ell^{(2)}$ corresponding to each leaf of $\mathcal{P}_\ell$ have been derived for $\ell = 0, \ldots, I-2$.

Let $C_{i,j}^{(v)}$ be a given claim in the portfolio, with at time I frequency feature $x_{i,j|\ell-j}^{(v)}$ and severity feature $\tilde{x}_{i,j|\ell-j}^{(v)}$, with $\ell = I - i$. The simulation procedure for the development cost of this claim is based on the following steps.

0. *Initialization.* Set:

$$\ell_0 = \ell, \quad K2_{i,j|\ell_0-j}^{(v)} = 0, \quad K2_{i,j|\ell_0-j}^{(v)} = 0, \quad \hat{x}_{i,j|\ell_0-j}^{(v)} = x_{i,j|\ell_0-j}^{(v)}, \quad \hat{\tilde{x}}_{i,j|\ell_0-j}^{(v)} = \tilde{x}_{i,j|\ell_0-j}^{(v)}.$$

1. Find the index r of the leaf of $\mathcal{P}_{\ell_0}$ to which the feature $\hat{x}_{i,j|\ell_0-j}^{(v)}$ belongs.

2. Simulate the state w of the frequency response $\widehat{W}_{i,j|\ell_0-j+1}^{(v)}$ at time $\ell_0 + i + 1$ using the probability distribution corresponding to the r-th leaf of $\mathcal{P}_{\ell_0}$.

3. If w implies:

   a. a type-1 payment (i.e., a NoCARD payment) at time $\ell_0 + i + 1$, then assume as the expected paid amount at time $\ell_0 + i + 1$ the estimate $\widehat{S1}_{i,j|\ell_0-j+1}^{(v)}$ corresponding to the leaf of $\mathcal{Q}_{\ell_0}^{(1)}$ to which the feature $\hat{\tilde{x}}_{i,j|\ell_0-j}^{(v)}$ belongs.

   b. a type-2 payment (i.e., a CARD payment) at time $\ell_0 + i + 1$, then assume as the expected paid amount at time $\ell_0 + i + 1$ the estimate $\widehat{S2}_{i,j|\ell_0-j+1}^{(v)}$ corresponding to the leaf of $\mathcal{Q}_{\ell_0}^{(2)}$ to which the feature $\hat{\tilde{x}}_{i,j|\ell_0-j}^{(v)}$ belongs.

   c. no payments at time $\ell_0 + i + 1$, then all payments at time $\ell_0 + i + 1$ are set to 0.

4. Set:
$$K1_{i,j|\ell_0-j+1}^{(v)} = K1_{i,j|\ell_0-j}^{(v)} + \widehat{S1}_{i,j|\ell_0-j+1}^{(v)}, \quad K2_{i,j|\ell_0-j+1}^{(v)} = K2_{i,j|\ell_0-j}^{(v)} + \widehat{S2}_{i,j|\ell_0-j+1}^{(v)}.$$

5. If $\ell_0 < I - 2$ then:

   5.1. The features $x_{i,j|\ell_0-j}^{(v)}$ and $\tilde{x}_{i,j|\ell_0-j}^{(v)}$ are updated with the new information provided by the responses $\widehat{W}_{i,j|\ell_0-j+1}^{(v)}, \widehat{S1}_{i,j|\ell_0-j+1}^{(v)}$ and $\widehat{S2}_{i,j|\ell_0-j+1}^{(v)}$, and the new features $\hat{x}_{i,j|\ell_0-j+1}^{(v)}$ and $\hat{\tilde{x}}_{i,j|\ell_0-j+1}^{(v)}$ are then obtained (this requires that the self-sustaining property holds).

   5.2. Set $\ell_0 = \ell_0 + 1$ and return to step 1.

With this procedure the two sample paths:

$$\left(K1_{i,j|\ell-j+\tau}^{(v)}\right)_{\tau=0,\ldots,I-1-\ell}, \quad \left(K2_{i,j|\ell-j+\tau}^{(v)}\right)_{\tau=0,\ldots,I-1-\ell},$$

of the type-1 and type-2 cumulated cost are simulated for the chosen claim $C_{i,j}^{(v)}$ with lag $\ell = I - i$. A simulation set of appropriate size is obtained with N independent iterations $h = 1, \ldots, N$ of this procedure. The cost estimates are then obtained as the costs on the average path, i.e.,:

$$\widehat{K1}_{i,j|\ell-j+\tau}^{(v)} = \frac{1}{N} \sum_{h=1}^{N} {}_h K1_{i,j|\ell-j+\tau}^{(v)},$$

$$\widehat{K2}_{i,j|\ell-j+\tau}^{(v)} = \frac{1}{N} \sum_{h=1}^{N} {}_h K2_{i,j|\ell-j+\tau}^{(v)},$$

$$\tau = 0, \ldots, I - 1 - \ell.$$

On the terminal date, i.e., for $\tau = I - 1 - \ell$, these sample averages provide the reserve estimates $E1_{i,j}^{(v)}$ and $E2_{i,j}^{(v)}$ in (18).

Once the CART approach has been extended to multiperiod predictions via simulation, it is convenient to make a further extension of the model to allow a joint dynamic modeling of the case reserves. Indeed, as anticipated in Section 5, to make the best use of the case reserve information in multiperiod predictions also the changes in the case reserve itself must be predicted by a specific model.

10.3. Including Dynamic Modeling of the Case Reserve

To dynamically model the case reserves, we extend the model assumptions in Section 4.2. Also, for the case reserve the conditional model is preferred, for the usual reason of a discrete probability mass typically present in 0 in the reserve distributions. Our additional assumptions are described as follows.

- The filtered probability space $(\Omega, \mathcal{F}, \mathbb{P}, \mathbb{F})$ must include also the two reserve processes:

$$(R1_{i,j|k}^{(v)})_{i,j,k,v}, \quad (R2_{i,j|k}^{(v)})_{i,j,k,v},$$

which are $\mathbb{F}$-adapted for $t = i + j + k$ and for which the independency assumptions (H1), (H2), (H3) also hold.

- For the distribution of the case reserves a property similar to assumption (H5) holds, i.e.,:

(HR5) For the conditional distribution of $R1_{i,j|k}^{(v)}|(\bar{R1}_{i,j|k}^{(v)} = 1)$ and $R2_{i,j|k}^{(v)}|(\bar{R2}_{i,j|k}^{(v)} = 1)$ one has:

$$\begin{aligned} R1_{i,j|k+1}^{(v)} \Big| \left(\bar{R1}_{i,j|k+1}^{(v)} = 1 \right) &\sim \mathcal{N}\left(\dot{\mu}_{j+k}^{(1)}(\dot{x}_{i,j|k}^{(v)}), \dot{\sigma}_1^2 \right), \\ R2_{i,j|k+1}^{(v)} \Big| \left(\bar{R2}_{i,j|k+1}^{(v)} = 1 \right) &\sim \mathcal{N}\left(\dot{\mu}_{j+k}^{(2)}(\dot{x}_{i,j|k}^{(v)}), \dot{\sigma}_2^2 \right), \end{aligned} \quad (20)$$

where $\dot{x}_{i,j|k}^{(v)} \in \mathcal{X}$ is a $\mathcal{F}_{i+j+k}$-measurable feature of $C_{i,j|k}^{(v)}$.

As for the payment variables, these assumptions imply:

$$\mathbb{E}\left[R1_{i,j|k+1}^{(v)} \Big| \mathcal{F}_{i+j+k}, \left(\bar{R1}_{i,j|k+1}^{(v)} = 1 \right) \right] = \dot{\mu}_{j+k}^{(1)}(\dot{x}_{i,j|k}^{(v)}),$$

$$\mathbb{E}\left[R2_{i,j|k+1}^{(v)} \Big| \mathcal{F}_{i+j+k}, \left(\bar{R2}_{i,j|k+1}^{(v)} = 1 \right) \right] = \dot{\mu}_{j+k}^{(2)}(\dot{x}_{i,j|k}^{(v)}),$$

where the conditional expectations can be calibrated by regression trees. Then there exists an $\mathcal{F}_{i+j+k}$-measurable severity feature $\tilde{x}_{i,j|k}^{(v)}$ which determines the conditional expectation of the cash flows $S1_{i,j|k}^{(v)}$ and $S2_{i,j|k}^{(v)}$. The unconditional reserve expectations are then given by:

$$\mathbb{E}\left[R1_{i,j|k+1}^{(v)} \Big| \mathcal{F}_{i+j+k} \right] = \dot{\mu}_{j+k}^{(1)}(\dot{x}_{i,j|k}^{(v)}) \, \mathbb{P}\left[\bar{R1}_{i,j|k+1}^{(v)} = 1 \Big| \mathcal{F}_{i+j+k} \right],$$

$$\mathbb{E}\left[R2_{i,j|k+1}^{(v)} \Big| \mathcal{F}_{i+j+k} \right] = \dot{\mu}_{j+k}^{(2)}(\dot{x}_{i,j|k}^{(v)}) \, \mathbb{P}\left[\bar{R2}_{i,j|k+1}^{(v)} = 1 \Big| \mathcal{F}_{i+j+k} \right].$$

- To further improve the predictive performance, an assumption similar to assumption (H4) or (H4′) can be added, which we express here in the one-dimensional form (8):

  (HR4′) For the conditional distribution of:

  $$\dot{W}^{(v)}_{i,j|k} = \bar{R}1^{(v)}_{i,j|k} + 2\bar{R}2^{(v)}_{i,j|k},$$

  one has:

  $$\dot{W}^{(v)}_{i,j|k+1} = w | \mathcal{F}_{i+j+k}, \left(Z^{(v)}_{i,j|k+1} = 0 \right) \sim \text{Categorical} \left(\dot{p}^{(w)}_{j+k} \left(x^{(v)}_{i,j|k} \right) \right), \quad (21)$$

  where $\dot{p}^{(w)}_{j+k} : \mathcal{X} \mapsto [0,1]^4$ is a probability function, i.e.:

  $$\sum_{w=0}^{3} \dot{p}^{(w)}_{j+k} \left(x^{(v)}_{i,j|k} \right) = 1.$$

  This assumption implies:

  $$\mathbb{P}\left[\dot{W}^{(v)}_{i,j|k+1} = w | \mathcal{F}_{i+j+k}, \left(Z^{(v)}_{i,j|k+1} = 0 \right) \right] = \dot{p}^{(w)}_{j+k} \left(x^{(v)}_{i,j|k} \right) \geq 0, \quad w = 0, \ldots, 3.$$

  Assumption (HR4′) is not required if there is only one type of payment, since if we have, say, only type-1 payments, then $\bar{R}1^{(v)}_{i,j|k+1} = 1 - Z^{(v)}_{i,j|k+1}$.

  We can consider additional conditioning in expression (20) and/or (21) in order to better modeling particular effects. For example, one could condition on the state of the indicator $Z^{(v)}_{i,j|k}$ at the previous date in order to distinguish predictions concerning open claims and reopened claims. All these enhancements of the model have been applied in the following examples.

10.4. Example of Simulated Cost Development Paths

Using the simulation procedure illustrated in Section 10.2 and the additional assumptions presented in the previous section we can provide examples of multiperiod predictions including the joint dynamic modeling of case reserves. We provide here an example of cost development path simulation for an individual claim, using the data on the same claims portfolio of examples in Section 8. Before considering a specific claim, we derived all the frequency and the severity partitions for all lags $\ell = 0, \ldots, 4$ by calibrating prediction trees on the entire claims portfolio. The run time of all these calibrations is roughly 3 min on a workstation with one 8-core Intel processor@3.60 GHz (4.30 GHz max turbo) and 32 GB RAM. We then considered an individual claim with the following characteristics:

- accident year: $i = I = 6$;
- reporting delay: $j = 0$, hence we denote the claim as $C^{(v)}_{6,0}$;
- the claim is open at time I: $Z^{(v)}_{6,0|0} = 0$;
- the claim does not involve a lawyer at time I: $L^{(v)}_{6,0|0} = 0$;
- no type-1 (NoCARD) payment made at time I: $S1^{(v)}_{6,0|0} = 0$;
- no type-2 (CARD) payment made at time I: $S2^{(v)}_{6,0|0} = 0$;
- type-1 reserve at time I: $R1^{(v)}_{6,0|0} = 31,460$ euros;
- type-2 reserve at time I: $R2^{(v)}_{6,0|0} = 13,820$ euros.

Since $i = I$ we start with $\ell_0 = 0$ in the simulation procedure, which provides the maximum length sample paths $\left(K1^{(v)}_{6,0|0}, K1^{(v)}_{6,0|1}, \ldots, K1^{(v)}_{6,0|5} \right)$ and $\left(K2^{(v)}_{6,0|0}, K2^{(v)}_{6,0|1}, \ldots, K2^{(v)}_{6,0|5} \right)$. In each simulation an execution of the predict.rpart function was invoked for each lag. The computation time required for simulating all sample paths (for the type-1 and type-2 cost) is roughly 4 min. In Figures 4 and 5 $N = 5000$ simulated sample paths for the type-1 and type-2 cumulated cost, respectively, of $C^{(v)}_{6,0}$ are reported. Since many paths overlap, the simulated paths are shown in blue with the color depth being proportional to the number of overlaps. The average paths in the two figures are shown in red: their final point corresponds to $\widehat{K1}_{6,0|5}^{(v)} = 17,069$ euros and $\widehat{K2}_{6,0|5}^{(v)} = 4314$ euros. If we assume that the claims are finalized at time 11, i.e., after $\tau = 5$ years for this claim, then these amounts can be taken as an estimate of the individual claim reserves $E1_{6,0}^{(v)}$ and $E2_{6,0}^{(v)}$ to be placed at the current date on $C_{6,0}^{(v)}$. This suggests significant decreases in both the outstanding case reserves, namely a decrease of 14,391 euros for $R1_{6,0|0}^{(v)}$ and a decrease of 7406 euros for $R2_{6,0|0}^{(v)}$.

It is interesting to note that with this dynamic approach we also have an estimate of the tail reserves $T1_{6,0}^{(v)}$ and $T2_{6,0}^{(v)}$ which are obtained as the average of the 5000 simulated values of $\widehat{R1}_{6,0|5}^{(v)}$ and $\widehat{R2}_{6,0|5}^{(v)}$. These estimates result in being $T1_{6,0}^{(v)} = 386$ euros and $T2_{6,0}^{(v)} = 248$ euros, which should be added to the corresponding expected cumulated costs, thus giving $E1_{6,0}^{(v)} = 17,455$ euros and $E2_{6,0}^{(v)} = 4562$ euros.

The variation coefficient in the simulated sample is 63.6% for type-1 reserve and 91.6% for type-2 reserve. The relative standard error of the mean is 0.9% and 1.3%, respectively.

Whether the reserve adjustments indicated by the model are actually done could depend on a specific decision. However, these findings should suggest putting the claim under scrutiny.

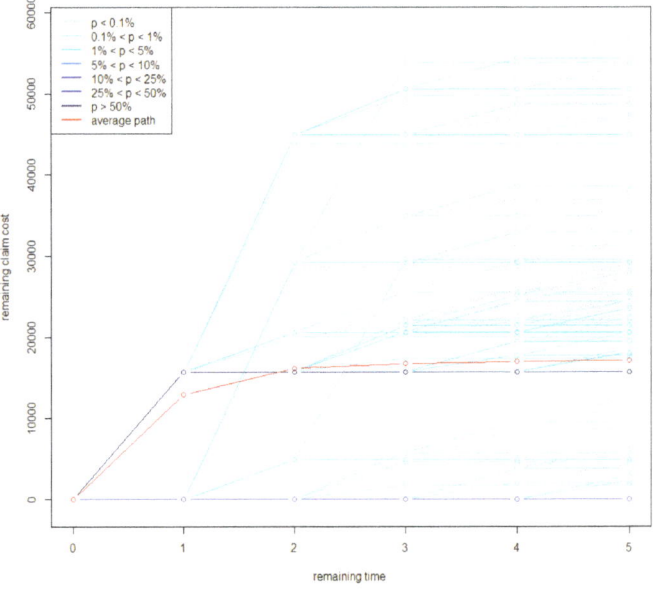

Figure 4. Representation of $N = 5000$ simulated paths for the type-1 cost development of the chosen claim $C_{6,0}^{(v)}$. In red the average path is reported.

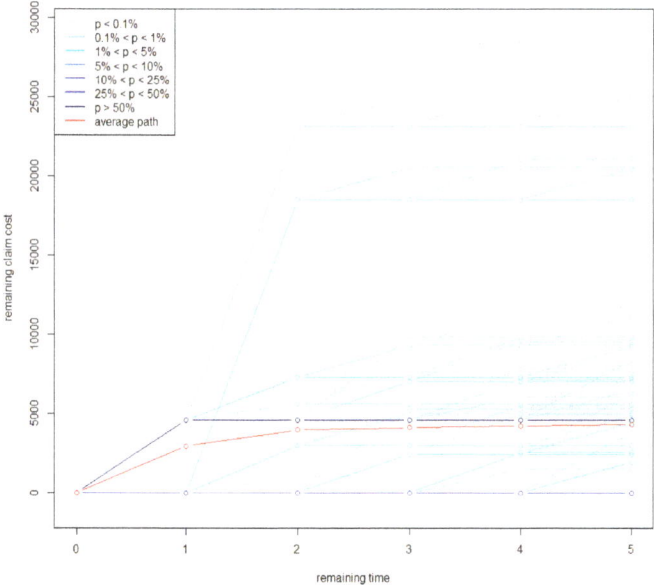

Figure 5. Representation of $N = 5000$ simulated paths for the type-2 cost development of the chosen claim $C_{6,0}^{(v)}$. The average path is in red.

11. Testing Predictive Performance of CART Approach

In this section, we propose some backtesting exercises in order to get some insight into the predictive performance of our CART approach. We first illustrate backtesting results for predictions of one-year event occurrences useful for claim watching. Multiperiod occurrence predictions could be similarly tested. Finally, we perform a typical claim reserving exercise, which is composed of two steps. In a first step the individual reserve estimate is derived by simulation for all the claims in the portfolio and the resulting total reserve (after the addition of an IBNYR reserve estimate) is compared with the classical chain-ladder reserve, which is estimated on aggregate payments at portfolio level. We perform these estimates on data deprived of the last calendar year observations. Then in a second step we can assess the predictive performance of the CART approach with respect to the chain-ladder approach by comparing the realized aggregate payments in the "first next diagonal" with those predicted by the two methods.

11.1. The Data

In these predictive efficiency tests, we need to calibrate the CART models assuming time $I - 1$ as the current date, since observations at time I are used to measure the forecast error. For this reason, data on claims portfolio used in the previous section has not sufficient historical depth. We then use in this section a different dataset containing a smaller variety of claim features (in particular, the variables $L_{i,j|k}^{(v)}$ are not present) but a longer observed claims history. We have:

- Observed accident years: from 2007 to 2016. Then $i = 1, \ldots, 10$.
- All claims reported are observed, hence for accident year i one has $j = 0, \ldots, 10 - i$ (i.e., $j_{-i} \equiv 0$).

Then there are 55 blocks (i, j) in the original dataset. The total number of reported claims is 1,337,329. However, since we use claims observed in year 2016 (i.e., responses with $i + j + k = 10$) for testing predictions, we assume $I = 9$ as the current date and we drop from the original dataset all claims with $i + j = 10$ and all observations with $i + j + k = 10$. This reduces the data for the calibration to 9 observed accident years (45 (i,j) blocks). In this data the pairs feature-response are observed for lags $\ell = 0, \ldots, I-3 = 7$. The total number of reported claims in this portfolio observed at time $I = 9$ is $\sum_{i,j} N_{i,j} = 1,211,392$. The number of observations in the calibration set and the prediction set of each lag is reported in Table 8.

Table 8. Number of observations in the calibration and the prediction set of each lag in the claims portfolio observed at time $I = 9$.

ℓ	$|\mathcal{D}_\ell^C|$	$|\mathcal{D}_\ell^P|$
0	1,012,099	121,633
1	964,302	119,075
2	852,271	116,207
3	732,116	121,885
4	592,538	139,828
5	445,686	146,965
6	296,880	148,895
7	144,310	152,593

11.2. Prediction of One-Year Event Occurrences

We test the predictive efficiency of some one-year event predictions considering the indicators of type-1 payment, type-2 payment and closure for lag $\ell = 0$, i.e., we consider the predicted responses $\widehat{Z}^{(v)}_{9,0|1}, \widehat{S1}^{(v)}_{9,0|1}, \widehat{S2}^{(v)}_{9,0|1}$ for $v = 1, \ldots, N_{9,0}$, i.e., for all the $|\mathcal{D}_0^P| = N_{9,0} = 121,633$ claims in block $(9,0)$. These response estimates were provided by the classification tree for the frequency calibrated on $\mathcal{D}_0^C$ (1,012,099 observations). Since these responses are actually observed at time 10, we can assess the predictive performance of the model by comparing predicted and realized values. To this aim, we refer to a specific forecasting exercise.

For a given indicator, let us denote as *positive*, or *negative*, a claim in the sample $\mathcal{D}_0^P$ for which the indicator will be 1, or 0, respectively. Our forecasting exercise consists of predicting not only how many claims in the sample will be positive, but also which of them will be positive. i.e., we want to provide the claim code cc of the Λ claims in the sample we predict as positive, where Λ is the number of claims we expect to be positive. Our prediction strategy is very intuitive. Let $\mathcal{R}_0^{(r)}$, $r = 1, \ldots, R_0$, the r-th leaf of the partition $\mathcal{P}_0$ provided by the calibrated frequency tree. Using notations introduced in Section 8.2, we denote by $n^{(r)}$ the number of claims belonging to $\mathcal{R}_0^{(r)}$ and by $\lambda^{(r)}$ the probability to be positive for each of these claims. We assume that the leaves are ordered by decreasing value of $\lambda^{(r)}$ and define $r^* = \min\{r : N^{(r)} \leq \Lambda\}$, where $N^{(r)} = \sum_{h=1}^{r} n^{(h)}$. Our forecasting strategy consists then in predicting as positive all the $N^{(r^*)}$ claims in the first r^* leaves and, in addition, $\Lambda - N^{(r^*)}$ claims which are randomly chosen among those in leaf $r^* + 1$.

The accuracy of our prediction could be measured by introducing an appropriate gain/loss function giving a specified (positive) score to claims correctly classified and a specified (negative) score to claims incorrectly classified. The choice of such a function, however, depends on the specific use one makes of the prediction, then in order to illustrate the results we prefer to resort here to the so-called *confusion matrices*, which we present in Figure 6. In these matrices blue (brown) cells refer to predicted (realized) values, green (red) cells refer to claims correctly (incorrectly) classified.

Let us consider, for example, the first matrix, concerning the indicator $\widehat{S1}^{(v)}_{9,0|1}$, i.e., {A type-1 payment is made in the next year}. We observe that 6581 claims of the 121,633 in the prediction set, i.e., the 5.4%, were predicted by the model to have a type-1 payment, while type-1 payments actually realized were 6966 (5.7%). Of the 6581 claims predicted as positive, 5209 resulted in being *true positive* (TP, green cell) and the remaining 1372 were *false positive* (FP, red cell). Considering the 115,052 claims predicted to have not a type-1 payment, i.e., to be negative, 1757 resulted in being *false negative* (FN, red cell) and the remaining 113,295 were *true negative* (TN, green cell). Then, globally, 118,504 claims were correctly predicted (97.4% of all the predicted claims) and the remaining 6966 were incorrectly predicted. Ratios typically used are also reported, as:

- *True positive ratio*, also known as *sensitivity*: TPR = TP/(TP+FN)= 74.8%;
- *True negative ratio*, or *specificity*: TNR = TN/(TN+FP)= 98.8%;
- *False negative ratio*: FNR = 1− TPR= 25.2%;
- *False positive ratio*: FPR = 1− TNR= 1.2%.

The other two matrices have the same structure.

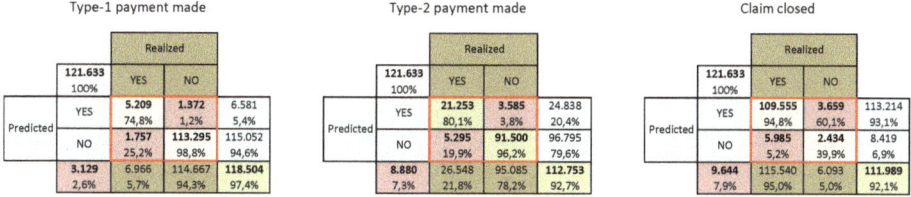

Figure 6. Confusion matrices for prediction of payment and closure indicators for claims with $\ell = 0$.

11.3. Prediction of Aggregate Claims Costs

11.3.1. Aggregate RBNS Reserve as Sum of Individual Reserves

We performed the CART calibration for the frequency-severity model extended with the dynamic case reserve model for all the 8 lags in the time-9 dataset. Given the large number of claims in this portfolio these calibrations required 73 min for computations. After the model calibration, for each of the 1,211,392 claims reported at time 9 we simulated $N = 50$ cost development paths for the type-1 and type-2 payments using the procedure illustrated in Section 10 and we computed the corresponding average paths. In each simulation and for each lag the predict.rpart function can be invoked only one time for all claims with the same lag. With respect to the simulation of a single claim, this provides, proportionally, a substantial reduction of computation time. The run time for all the simulations was roughly 120 min.

By computing the incremental payments of each average path and summing over the entire portfolio we obtained a CART reserve estimate for the reported but not settled (RBNS) claims. If these total payments are organized by accident year (on the rows) and payment date (on the column) we obtain a "lower triangle" of estimated future payments with the same structure of the usual lower triangles in classical claims reserving.

By the simulation procedure the individual reserve estimates are provided:

$$\widehat{K1}_{i,j|8-j}^{(v)} = \frac{1}{N}\sum_{h=1}^{N} {}_hK1_{i,j|8-j}^{(v)},$$

$$\widehat{K2}_{i,j|8-j}^{(v)} = \frac{1}{N}\sum_{h=1}^{N} {}_hK2_{i,j|8-j}^{(v)},$$

$$\widehat{K}_{i,j|8-j}^{(v)} = \widehat{K1}_{i,j|8-j}^{(v)} + \widehat{K2}_{i,j|8-j}^{(v)},$$

$$i = 2, \ldots, 9,\ j = 0, \ldots 9 - i,\ v = 1, \ldots, N_{i,j}.$$

Assuming claims finalization at time $2I - 1 = 17$, one obtains from these cost estimates the corresponding RBNS reserves, at different levels of aggregation:

$$E1_i^{RBNS} := \sum_{j=0}^{9-i}\sum_{v=1}^{N_{i,j}} \widehat{K1}_{i,j|8-j}^{(v)}, \quad i=2,\ldots,I; \qquad E1^{RBNS} = \sum_{i=2}^{9} E1_i^{RBNS};$$

$$E2_i^{RBNS} := \sum_{j=0}^{9-i}\sum_{v=1}^{N_{i,j}} \widehat{K2}_{i,j|8-j}^{(v)}, \quad i=2,\ldots,I; \qquad E2^{RBNS} = \sum_{i=2}^{9} E2_i^{RBNS}; \qquad (22)$$

$$E^{RBNS} = E1^{RBNS} + E1^{RBNS}.$$

The simulation procedure also provides the individual tail reserve estimates:

$$\widehat{R1}_{i,j|8-j}^{(v)} = \frac{1}{N}\sum_{h=1}^{N} {}_h\widehat{R1}_{i,j|8-j}^{(v)},$$

$$\widehat{R2}_{i,j|8-j}^{(v)} = \frac{1}{N}\sum_{h=1}^{N} {}_h\widehat{R2}_{i,j|8-j}^{(v)},$$

$$\widehat{R}_{i,j|8-j}^{(v)} = \widehat{R1}_{i,j|8-j}^{(v)} + \widehat{R2}_{i,j|8-j}^{(v)},$$

$$i=1,\ldots,9, \; j=0,\ldots 9-i, \; v=1,\ldots,N_{i,j},$$

which can be aggregated as:

$$T1_i = \sum_{j=0}^{9-i}\sum_{v=1}^{N_{i,j}} \widehat{R1}_{i,j|8-j}^{(v)}, \quad i=1,\ldots,I; \qquad T1 = \sum_{i=1}^{9} T1_i;$$

$$T2_i = \sum_{j=0}^{9-i}\sum_{v=1}^{N_{i,j}} \widehat{R2}_{i,j|8-j}^{(v)}, \quad i=1,\ldots,I; \qquad T2 = \sum_{i=1}^{9} T2_i;$$

$$T = T1 + T2.$$

These estimates can be added to the corresponding estimates in (22) in order to provide an adjustment of the reserves computed under the assumption of finalization at time $2I-1$.

As usual, the aggregate claim cost estimates can be organized by accident year and by *development year* (dy), indexed as $h=0,\ldots,I-1$, where in the CART model "development year" is a new wording for the "lag" $I+\tau-i$. With this representation we obtain the "lower triangle" for the total costs (type 1 + type 2) reported in Table 9 in green color.

Table 9. Aggregate lower triangle of the incremental RBNS cost estimates and corresponding RBNS reserves. In the last two rows the adjustments for IBNYR claims are reported.

ay i	dy = 1	dy = 2	dy = 3	dy = 4	dy = 5	dy = 6	dy = 7	dy = 8	reserve: E_i^{RBNS}	CoVa$_i$
1	.	.	.	.	.	.	.	.	0	0.00%
2	.	.	.	.	.	.	.	548,939	548,939	5.51%
3	.	.	.	.	.	.	841,939	660,135	1,502,074	9.12%
4	.	.	.	.	.	1,336,090	989,338	679,961	3,005,388	5.50%
5	.	.	.	.	1,989,568	1,352,147	1,026,083	663,033	5,030,831	6.18%
6	.	.	.	2,652,175	1,842,702	1,266,884	799,521	595,623	7,156,905	3.63%
7	.	.	4,658,838	2,609,709	1,584,964	1,170,623	725,353	569,174	11,318,662	2.97%
8	.	10,672,731	4,061,362	2,479,849	1,849,869	1,104,580	693,130	543,766	21,405,288	1.66%
9	32,184,296	7,479,426	3,467,081	2,644,659	1,819,141	1,158,269	685,487	593,554	50,031,913	1.11%
RBNS diagonal	54,884,575	18,994,820	10,504,823	7,127,705	4,244,697	2,420,573	1,229,253	593,554	100,000,000	0.79%
IBNYR	5,393,583	1,416,003	688,614	518,063	341,608	220,980	126,677	95,314	8,800,841	
RBNS+IBNYR	60,278,158	20,410,822	11,193,436	7,645,768	4,586,305	2,641,554	1,355,930	688,868	108,800,841	

Figures in the aggregate "upper triangle" (pink color) are not reported in order to point out that this kind of data were not used for the prediction. Total estimated costs summed by diagonal (highlighted by different green intensity) as well as summed by accident year (second last column) are also reported. For confidentiality reasons all paid amounts in this numerical example were rescaled so as to obtain a total reserve $E^{RBNS} = 100,000,000$ euros. For each accident year reserve estimate and for the total estimate the coefficient of variation on the simulated sample was computed. These figures, reported in the last column of the table, are rather low. This should be explained by the fact that each aggregate reserve simulation is the sum of a very large number of individual claim costs and the correlation among these individual costs is very low. Obviously, this weak correlation is also a consequence of the independence assumptions in the model.

11.3.2. Inclusion of the IBNYR Reserve Estimate

We are interested in comparing the CART reserve estimates with the classical chain-ladder reserve estimates. To allow this comparison a cost estimate for IBNYR claims must be added to the aggregate RBNS reserve derived in the previous section. Therefore, we complemented the RBNS reserve model with an ancillary model for the IBNYR reserve, which is outlined in Appendix A. This model is a "severity extension" of the "frequency approach" proposed in Wüthrich (2016) for estimating the expected number of IBNYR claims. The results of the ancillary model estimates are summarized (after rescaling) in the second last row of Table 9, where the IBNYR reserves, by diagonal and overall, are reported. Figures in the last row provide the corresponding RBNS claim reserves adjusted for IBNYR claims.

Remark 5. *This separation between RBNS and IBNYR claims is in some respect similar to that obtained in Verral et al. (2010).*

11.3.3. Comparison with Chain-Ladder Estimates

In the chain-ladder approach to classical claims reserving the sums of all the individual claim payments in the portfolio observed up to time I are organized by accident year and development year and an upper triangle of observed paid losses, cumulated along development in each accident year, is obtained. The reserve estimates are then derived by the cumulated paid losses in the lower triangle, which is obtained by applying to the upper triangle the well-known chain-ladder algorithm. This is shown in Table 10 where, to allow comparison with Table 9, incremental payments are reported.

Table 10. Chain-ladder reserve estimates on aggregate payments (type-1+type-2, incremental figures). The differences with the CARTs estimates are also reported.

ay i	dy = 0	dy = 1	dy = 2	dy = 3	dy = 4	dy = 5	dy = 6	dy = 7	dy = 8	Reserve E_i^{CL}
1	35,699,311	37,879,857	12,003,345	6,478,312	3,033,793	1,895,577	1,026,086	922,252	497,792	0
2	41,730,803	36,146,954	14,363,454	4,928,858	3,051,338	2,913,180	1,237,083	899,977	529,656	529,656
3	40,033,745	31,396,571	13,499,535	5,668,671	2,719,742	2,314,666	856,136	868,753	489,839	1,358,592
4	39,027,439	38,571,568	12,499,545	6,084,483	2,903,344	2,930,986	1,075,959	928,216	523,367	2,527,541
5	39,143,444	37,227,132	11,612,033	4,676,458	2,897,767	2,477,989	1,033,956	891,980	502,936	4,906,860
6	33,900,305	33,987,815	11,872,716	5,088,186	2,644,290	2,268,885	946,706	816,711	460,496	7,137,087
7	31,820,892	33,590,427	10,841,703	4,822,608	2,526,694	2,167,983	904,604	780,390	440,016	11,642,296
8	33,667,137	32,084,528	11,173,371	4,865,109	2,548,961	2,187,090	912,576	787,268	443,894	22,918,269
9	39,151,374	37,275,145	12,987,380	5,654,965	2,962,788	2,542,166	1,060,734	915,081	515,961	63,914,221
CL diagonal	.	60,867,772	25,100,078	12,733,962	7,374,128	4,695,628	2,288,018	1,358,976	515,961	114,934,523
CL—CARTs	.	589,614	4,689,256	1,540,526	−271,640	109,323	−353,535	3,046	−172,907	6,133,683
%	.	1.0%	23.0%	13.8%	−3.6%	2.4%	−13.4%	0.2%	−25.1%	5.6%

As in Table 9 the upper triangle is highlighted in pink and the lower triangle in green, and the chain-ladder reserves at different aggregation levels—by diagonal, by accident year, overall—are computed. In the last two rows of the table the differences with the CART estimates in the last row of Table 9 are shown. In some diagonals, i.e., in some future calendar years, there are substantial differences between the chain-ladder and the CART claims cost predictions. However, the overall chain-ladder reserve estimate is 5.6% higher than the corresponding CART estimate. When the results provided by the two methods are compared, one should take into account that the chain-ladder estimates do include an underwriting year inflation forecast, since an estimate of historical underwriting year inflation is implicitly projected on future dates by the algorithm. In the CART approach, instead, some degree of expected inflation might be implicitly included in the predicted costs only through the case reserves. An additional component of expected inflation must however be added to the reserve estimates. A similar problem is found in DCL model, see Martínez-Miranda et al. (2013) for an estimation method of the underwriting year inflation based on incurred data.

11.3.4. Backtesting the Two Methods on the Next Diagonal

Since we deliberately made the reserve estimates for a claims portfolio observed at time 10 (i.e., 2016) using only data observed up to time 9 (2015), we are now able to perform a backtest on the "first next diagonal" since next-year realized payments (of both type 1 and type 2) are actually known. In Table 11 the realized payments and the prediction errors (i.e., realized − predicted) of the two methods are reported for accident years $2 \leq i \leq 9$.

Table 11. Forecast errors of CARTs and chain-ladder method on the next-year claim payments.

ay: i	Realized Payments	Chain-ladder Error	(%)	CART Error	(%)
2 (2008)	586,099	−56,443	−9.63	−37,109	−6.33
3 (2009)	1,145,117	−276,364	−24.13	−284,528	−24.85
4 (2010)	2,272,564	−1,196,605	−52.65	−916,852	−40.34
5 (2011)	1,734,932	743,057	42.83	279,561	16.11
6 (2012)	3,129,167	−484,877	−15.50	−445,027	−14.22
7 (2013)	3,902,228	920,380	23.59	872,408	22.36
8 (2014)	10,637,406	535,965	5.04	394,152	3.71
9 (2015)	38,117,533	−842,388	−2.21	−1,109,494	−2.91
total	61,525,046	−657,275	−1.07	−1,246,889	−2.03

The backtest exercise shows important errors in some accident years for both the methods. The overall predictions, however, are rather good for the two methods, showing an under-estimate of 1.07% by chain-ladder and 2.03% by CARTs. Considering possible adjustments for the expected inflation of CART prediction, we can say that in this case the predictive accuracy of the two methods is roughly similar.

Remark 6. *In this backtesting exercise the chain-ladder method has good predictive performance on the total reserve and is not easy to improve. A better assessment of the predictive efficiency of the CART approach in providing estimates of the aggregate reserve as sum of individual reserves could be obtained in cases where the chain-ladder approach poorly performs. For example, repeating the same exercise on different claims data (which for the moment are not authorized for disclosure), we observed on the total reserve estimate a forecast error of 18.64% with the chain-ladder and −5.10% with the CART approach.*

12. Conclusions

The CART approach illustrated in this paper seems promising for claims reserving and, more generally, for the claim watching activity. The large model flexibility of CARTs allows inclusion in the model of effects in the claims development process, which are difficult to study with classical methods. CARTs are rather efficient also in variable selection. However, the role of expert opinions in the choice of the explanatory variables to be included in the model is still important. Also, in this respect the interpretability of the results provided by CARTs can be very helpful.

Prediction and claims handling methods provided by the CART approach can also have an impact on business organization, in so far as they suggest and promote a closer connection into the insurance firm between the actuarial and the claims settlement activity.

As usual, the reliability of the results depends crucially on the quality of data available. In the proposed CART applications, it is also true, however, that enlarging the richness of data can also extend the scope and the significance of the results. For example, if information at individual policy level is included in the dataset, our CART approach could also provide indications useful for non-life-insurance pricing.

As is well known, a main disadvantage of CARTs is that they are not very robust towards changes in the data, since a small change in the observations may lead to a largely different optimal tree. Also, the sensitivity of the optimal tree to changes of the calibration parameters should be carefully analyzed. Random forests are proposed as the natural answer to the instability problem; however, the interpretability of the results is an important property which should not be lost. Backtesting exercises as those presented in this paper could help to get the instability effects under control.

Author Contributions: Both authors contributed equally to this work.

Funding: This research received no external funding.

Acknowledgments: We would like to kindly thank Gaia Montanucci and Matteo Salciarini (Alef) for their help in the preparation of data and the fine tuning of the calculation engines.

Conflicts of Interest: The authors declare no conflict of interest.

Appendix A. An Ancillary Model for the Estimation of IBNYR Reserve

For the sake of brevity, we formulate the model for the IBNYR reserve referring only to type-1 payments. By the model assumptions presented in Section 4.2 the aggregate RBNS reserve estimate is given by:

$$E1^{RBNS} = \sum_{i=2}^{I} \sum_{j=0}^{I-i} \sum_{k>I-(i+j)} \sum_{v=1}^{N_{i,j}} \mathbb{E}\left[S1_{i,j|k}^{(v)} \Big| \mathcal{F}_I\right].$$

If the process $(N_{i,j})_{i,j}$ were deterministic, the aggregate IBNYR reserve estimate could be written as:

$$E1^{IBNYR} = \sum_{i=2}^{I} \sum_{j=I-i+1}^{J} \sum_{v=1}^{N_{i,j}} \sum_{k \geq 0} \mathbb{E}\left[S1_{i,j|k}^{(v)} \Big| \mathcal{F}_I\right].$$

The process $(N_{i,j})_{i,j}$, however, is $\mathbb{F}$-adapted at time $i+j$, therefore the values of N_{ij} in the sum by j are not known at time I. Under proper assumptions (see Wüthrich 2016; Verrall and Wüthrich 2016) the IBNYR reserve can be estimated as:

$$E1^{IBNYR} = \sum_{i=2}^{I} \sum_{j=I-i+1}^{J} \mathbb{E}\left[N_{i,j}\big|\mathcal{F}_I\right] \mathbb{E}\left[\sum_{k \geq 0} S1_{i,j|k}^{(v)}\right],$$

where:

- the conditional expectation $\mathbb{E}\left[N_{i,j}\big|\mathcal{F}_I\right]$ is given by an estimate $\widehat{N}_{i,j}^{CL}$ obtained by chain-ladder techniques applied to the aggregate number of reported claims;
- the expectation $\mathbb{E}\left[\sum_{k \geq 0} S1_{i,j|k}^{(v)}\right]$ of the total cost for claims with reporting delay j is given by an estimate $\widehat{c}_j$ obtained with the CART approach for the RBNS claims. Assuming that claims in different accident years are identically distributed one has:

$$\widehat{c}_j = \frac{1}{I-j} \sum_{i=1}^{I-j} \frac{1}{N_{i,j}} \sum_{v=1}^{N_{i,j}} \widehat{S1}_{i,j}^{(v)},$$

where:

$$\widehat{S1}_{i,j}^{(v)} = \sum_{k=0}^{I-(i+j)} S1_{i,j|k}^{(v)} + \sum_{k>I-(i+j)} \widehat{\mathbb{E}}\left[S1_{i,j|k}^{(v)}\big|\mathcal{F}_I\right],$$

is the total cost estimated for claim $\mathcal{C}_{i,j}^{(v)}$.

The (type-1) IBNYR reserve estimate is then obtained as:

$$E1^{IBNYR} = \sum_{i=2}^{I} \sum_{j=I-i+1}^{J} \widehat{N}_{i,j}^{CL} \widehat{c}_j.$$

References

Breiman, Leo, Jerome H. Friedman, Richard A. Olshen, and Charles J. Stone. 1998. *Classification and Regression Trees*. London: Chapman & Hall/CRC.

D'Agostino, Luca, Massimo De Felice, Gaia Montanucci, Franco Moriconi, and Matteo Salciarini. 2018. *Machine learning per la riserva sinistri individuale. Un'applicazione R.C. Auto degli alberi di classificazione e regressione*. Alef Technical Reports No. 18/02. Available online: http://alef.it/doc/TechRep_18_02.pdf (accessed on 9 Octrober 2019).

Gabrielli, Andrea, Richman, Ronald, and Mario V. Wüthrich. 2018. Neural network embedding of the over-dispersed Poisson reserving model. *Scandinavian Actuaria Journal* 1–29. [CrossRef]

Hastie, Trevor, Robert Tibshirani, and Jerome Friedman. 2008. *The Elements of Statistical Learning. Data Mining, Inference, and Predictions*, 2nd ed. Springer Series in Statistics. Berlin: Springer.

Hiabu, Munir, Carolin Margraf, Maria Dolores Martínez-Miranda, and Jens Perch Nielsen. 2015. The link between classical reserving and granular reserving through double chain ladder and its extensions. *British Actuarial Journal* 21: 97–116. [CrossRef]

Martinez-Miranda, Maria Dolores, Bent Nielsen, Jens Perch Nielsen, and Richard Verrall. 2011. Cash Flow Simulation for a Model of Outstanding Liabilities Based on Claim Amounts and Claim Numbers. *Astin Bulletin* 41: 107–29.

Martínez-Miranda, Maria Dolores, Jens Perch Nielsen, and Richard Verrall. 2012. Double Chain Ladder. *ASTIN Bulletin* 42: 59–76.

Martínez-Miranda, Maria Dolores, Jens Perch Nielsen, and Richard Verrall. 2013. Double Chain Ladder and Bornhuetter-Ferguson. *North American Actuarial Journal* 17: 101–13. [CrossRef]

Pešta, Michal, and Ostap Okhrin. 2014. Conditional least squares and copulae in claims reserving for a single line of business. *Insurance: Mathematics and Economics* 56: 28–37. [CrossRef]

Taylor, Greg. 2019. *Claim Models: Granular and Machine Learning Forms*. Sydney: School of Risk and Actuarial Studies, University of South Wales.

Taylor, Greg, Gráinne McGuire, and James Sullivan. 2008. Individual claim loss reserving conditioned by case estimates. *Annals of Actuarial Science* 3: 215–56. [CrossRef]

Therneau, Terry M., Elizabeth J. Atkinson, and Mayo Foundation. 2015. *An Introduction to Recursive Partitioning Using the RPART Routines*. R Vignettes, version of June 29. Rochester: Mayo Foundation.

Verrall, Richard, Jens Perch Nielsen, and Anders Hedegaard Jessen. 2010. Prediction of RBNS and IBNR claims using claim amounts and claim counts. *ASTIN Bulletin* 40: 871–87.

Verrall, Richard J., and Mario V. Wüthrich. 2016. Understanding reporting delay in general insurance. *Risks* 4: 25. [CrossRef]

Wüthrich, Mario V. 2016. *Machine Learning in Individual Claims Reserving*. Research Paper No. 16-67. Zürich: Swiss Finance Institute.

Wüthrich, Mario V., and Christoph Buser. 2019. *Data Analytics for Non-Life Insurance Pricing*. Research Paper No. 16-68. Zürich: Swiss Finance Institute. Available online: https://ssrn.com/abstract=2870308 (accessed on 9 October 2019).

Wüthrich, Mario V., and Michael Merz. 2019. Editorial: Yes, we CANN! *ASTIN Bulletin* 49: 1–3. [CrossRef]

© 2019 by the authors. Licensee MDPI, Basel, Switzerland. This article is an open access article distributed under the terms and conditions of the Creative Commons Attribution (CC BY) license (http://creativecommons.org/licenses/by/4.0/).

Article

Individual Loss Reserving Using a Gradient Boosting-Based Approach

Francis Duval [†] and Mathieu Pigeon [*,†]

Quantact/Département de Mathématiques, Université du Québec à Montréal (UQAM), Montreal, QC H2X 3Y7, Canada
* Correspondence: pigeon.mathieu.2@uqam.ca
† These authors contributed equally to this work.

Received: 30 May 2019; Accepted: 5 July 2019; Published: 12 July 2019

Abstract: In this paper, we propose models for non-life loss reserving combining traditional approaches such as Mack's or generalized linear models and gradient boosting algorithm in an individual framework. These claim-level models use information about each of the payments made for each of the claims in the portfolio, as well as characteristics of the insured. We provide an example based on a detailed dataset from a property and casualty insurance company. We contrast some traditional aggregate techniques, at the portfolio-level, with our individual-level approach and we discuss some points related to practical applications.

Keywords: loss reserving; predictive modeling; individual models; gradient boosting

1. Introduction and Motivation

In its daily practice, a non-life insurance company is subject to a number of solvency constraints, e.g., ORSA guidelines in North America and Solvency II in Europe. More specifically, an actuary must predict, with the highest accuracy, future claims based on past observations. The difference between the total predicted amount and the total of all amounts already paid represents a reserve that the company must set aside. Much of the actuarial literature is devoted to the modeling, evaluation and management of this risk, see Wüthrich and Merz (2008) for an overview of existing methods.

Almost all existing models can be divided into two categories depending on the granularity of the underlying dataset: individual (or micro-level) approaches, when most information on contracts, claims, payments, etc. has been preserved, and collective (or macro-level) approaches involving some form of aggregation (often on an annual basis). The latter have been widely developed by researchers and successfully applied by practitioners for several decades. In contrast, individual approaches have been studied for decades but are currently used rarely despite the many advantages of these methods.

The idea of using an individual model for claims dates back to the early 1980s with, among others, Bühlmann et al. (1980), Hachemeister (1980) and Norberg (1986). The latter author has proposed an individual model describing the occurrence, the reporting delay and the severity of each claim separately. The idea was followed by the work of Arjas (1989), Norberg (1993, 1999), Hesselager (1994), Jewell (1989) and Haastrup and Arjas (1996). This period was characterized by very limited computing and memory resources as well as by the lack of usable data on individual claims. However, we can find some applications in Haastrup and Arjas (1996) and in some more technical documents.

Since the beginning of the 2000s, several studies have been done including, among others, the modeling of dependence using copulas Zhao and Zhou (2010), the use of generalized linear models Larsen (2007), the semi-parametric modeling of certain components Antonio and Plat (2014) and Zhao et al. (2009), the use of skew-symmetric distributions Pigeon et al. (2014), the inclusion of additional information Taylor et al. (2008), etc. Finally, some researchers have done comparisons between individual and collective approaches, often attempting to answer the question "what is the best approach?" (see Hiabu et al. (2016); Huang et al. (2015) or Charpentier and Pigeon (2016) for some examples).

Today, statistical learning techniques are widely used in the field of data analytics and may offer non-parametric solutions to claim reserving. These methods give the model more freedom and often outperform the accuracy of their parametric counterparts. However, only few approaches have been developed using micro-level information. One of them is presented in Wüthrich (2018), where the number of payments is modeled using regression trees in a discrete time framework. The occurrence of a claim payment is assumed to have a Bernoulli distribution, and the probability is then computed using a regression tree as well as all available characteristics. Other researchers, see Baudry and Robert (2017), have also developed a non-parametric approach using a machine learning algorithm known as extra-trees, an ensemble of many unpruned regression trees, for loss reserving. Finally, some researchers consider neural networks to improve classical loss reserving models (see Gabrielli et al. (2019)).

In this paper, we propose and analyze an individual model for loss reserving based on an application of a gradient boosting algorithm. Gradient boosting is a machine learning technique, that combines many "simple" models called weak learners to form a stronger predictor by optimizing some objective function. We apply an algorithm called XGBoost, see Chen and Guestrin (2016), but other machine learning techniques, such as an Extra-Trees algorithm, could also be considered.

Our strategy is to directly predict the ultimate claim amount of a file using all available information at a given time. Our approach is different from the one proposed in Wüthrich (2018) where regression trees (CART) are used to model the total number of payments per claim and/or the total amount paid per claim for each of the development periods. It is also different from the model proposed in Baudry and Robert (2017), which works recursively to build the full development of a claim, period after period.

We also present and analyze micro-level models belonging to the class of generalized linear models (GLM). Based on a detailed dataset from a property and casualty insurance company, we study some properties and we compare results obtained from various approaches. More specifically, we show that the approach combining the XGBoost algorithm and a classical collective model such as Mack's model, has high predictive power and stability. We also propose a method for dealing with censored data and discuss the presence of dynamic covariates. We believe that the gradient boosting algorithm could be an interesting addition to the range of tools available for actuaries to evaluate the solvency of a portfolio. This case study also enriches the too short list of analyzes based on datasets from insurance companies.

In Section 2, we introduce the notation and we present the context of loss reserving from both collective and individual point of view. In Section 3, we define models based on both, generalized linear models and gradient boosting algorithm. A case study and some numerical analyses on a detailed dataset are performed in Section 4, and finally, we conclude and present some promising generalizations in Section 5.

2. Loss Reserving

In non-life insurance, a claim always starts with an accident experienced by a policyholder that may lead to financial damages covered by an insurance contract. We call the date on which the accident happens the occurrence point (T_1). For some situations (bodily injury liability coverage, accident benefits, third-party responsibility liability, etc.), a reporting delay is observed between the occurrence point and the notification to the insurer at the reporting point (T_2). From T_2, the insurer could observe details about the accident, as well as some information about the insured, and record a first estimation of the final amount, called case estimate. Once the accident is reported to the insurance company, the claim is usually not settled immediately, e.g., the insurer has to investigate the case or to wait for bills or court judgments. At the reporting point T_2, a series of M random payments $P_{t_1}, \ldots, P_{t_M}$ made respectively at times $t_1 < \ldots < t_M$ is therefore triggered, until the claim is closed at the settlement point (T_3). To simplify the presentation, all dates are expressed in number of years from an ad hoc starting point denoted by τ. Finally, we need a unique index k, $k = 1, \ldots, K$, to distinguish the accidents. For instance, $T_1^{(k)}$ is the occurrence date of the accident k, and $t_m^{(k)}$ is the date of the mth payment of this claim. Figure 1 illustrates the development of a claim.

The evaluation date t^* is the moment on which the insurance company wants to evaluate its solvency and calculate its reserves. At this point, a claim can be classified in three categories:

1. If $T_1^{(k)} < t^* < T_2^{(k)}$, the accident has happened but has not yet been reported to the insurer. It is therefore called an "incurred but not reported" (IBNR), claim. For one of those claims, the insurer does not have specific information about the accident, but can use policyholder and external information to estimate the reserve.
2. If $T_2^{(k)} < t^* < T_3^{(k)}$, the accident has been reported to the insurer but is still not settled, which means the insurer expects to make additional payments to the insured. It is therefore called a "reported but not settled" (RBNS), claim. For one such claim, the historical information as well as policyholder and external information can be used to estimate the reserve.
3. If $t^* > T_3^{(k)}$, the claim is classified as settled, or S, and the insurer does not expect to make more payments.

Finally, it is always possible for a claim to reopen after its settlement point T_3.

Let $C_t^{(k)}$ be a random variable representing the cumulative paid amount at date t for claim k:

$$C_t^{(k)} = \begin{cases} 0, & t < T_2^{(k)} \\ \sum_{\{m: t_m^{(k)} \leq t\}} P_{t_m^{(k)}}, & t \geq T_2^{(k)}. \end{cases}$$

At any evaluation date $T_1^{(k)} < t^* < T_3^{(k)}$ and for an accident k, an insurer wants to predict the cumulative paid amount at the settlement $C_{T_3}^{(k)}$, called total paid amount, by $\widehat{C}_{T_3}^{(k)}$ using all information available at t^* and denoted by $\mathcal{D}_{t^*}^{(k)}$. The individual reserve for a claim evaluated at t^* is then given by $\widehat{R}_{t^*}^{(k)} = \widehat{C}_{T_3}^{(k)} - C_{t^*}^{(k)}$. For the whole portfolio, the total reserve is the aggregation of all individual reserves and is given by

$$\widehat{R}_{t^*} = \sum_{k=1}^{K} \widehat{R}_{t^*}^{(k)}.$$

Traditionally, insurance companies aggregate information by accident year and by development year. Claims with accident year i, $i = 1, \ldots, I$, are all the claims that occurred in the ith year after τ, which means all claims k for which $i - 1 < T_1^{(k)} < i$ is verified. For a claim k, a payment made in development year j, $j = 1, \ldots, J = I$ is a payment made in the jth year after the occurrence $T_1^{(k)}$, namely a payment $P_{t_m^{(k)}}$ for which $j - 1 < t_m^{(k)} - T_1^{(k)} < j$. For development years $j = 1, \ldots, I$, we define

$$Y_j^{(k)} = \sum_{m \in \mathcal{S}_j^{(k)}} P_{t_m^{(k)}},$$

where $\mathcal{S}_j^{(k)} = \{m : j - 1 < t_m^{(k)} - T_1^{(k)} < j\}$, as the total paid amount for claim k during year j and we define the corresponding cumulative paid amount as

$$C_j^{(k)} = \sum_{s=1}^{j} Y_s^{(k)}.$$

The collective group approaches every claim in the same accident year to form the aggregate incremental payment

$$Y_{ij} = \sum_{k \in \mathcal{K}_i} Y_j^{(k)}, \quad i,j = 1,\ldots,I,$$

where $\mathcal{K}_i$ is the set of all claims with accident year i. For portfolio-level models, a prediction of the reserve at time t^* is obtained by

$$\widehat{R}_{t^*} = \sum_{i=2}^{I} \sum_{j=I+2-i}^{I} \widehat{Y}_{ij}, \tag{1}$$

where the $\widehat{Y}_{ij}$ are usually predicted using only the accident year and the development year.

Each cell contains a series of payments, information about the claims and some information about policyholders. These payments can also be modeled within an individual framework. Hence, a prediction of the total reserve amount is given by

$$\widehat{R}_{t^*} = \underbrace{\sum_{i=2}^{I} \sum_{j=I+2-i}^{I} \sum_{k \in \mathcal{K}_i} \widehat{Y}_j^{(k)}}_{\text{RBNS reserve}} + \underbrace{\sum_{i=2}^{I} \sum_{j=I+2-i}^{I} \sum_{k \in \mathcal{K}_i^{\text{unobs.}}} \widehat{Y}_j^{(k)}}_{\text{IBNR reserve}}, \tag{2}$$

where $\mathcal{K}_i^{\text{unobs.}}$ is the set of IBNR claims with occurrence year i and the $\widehat{Y}_j^{(k)}$ can now be predicted using all available information. It should be noted that in Equations (1) and (2), we assume that all claims are paid for the earliest occurrence period ($i = 1$). In this paper, we adopt this point of view and we mainly focus on estimating the RBNS reserve, which is the first part on the right-hand side of Equation (2).

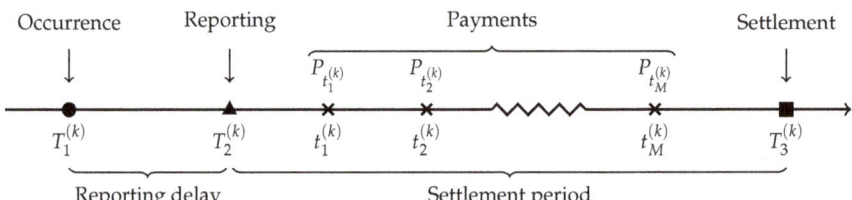

Figure 1. Development of claim k.

3. Models for Loss Reserving

3.1. Bootstrap Mack's Model and Generalized Linear Models for Loss Reserving

In Section 4, we compare our micro-level approach with three different types of models for loss reserving: a bootstrapped Mack's model England and Verrall (2002), a collective GLM Wüthrich and Merz (2008) and an individual version of the latter. In order to enrich the discussion that will be done in the analysis, we briefly present in this subsection these three different approaches.

Mack's model Mack (1993) is a distribution-free stochastic loss reserving method built for a cumulative run-off triangle. This collective model is among the most popular for loss reserving and as a result, the literature is more than substantial about it. One of the main drawbacks of this technique is that the predictive distribution of the total reserve cannot be computed directly due to the absence of a distribution assumption. In order to compare with our gradient boosting approach, we thus use a bootstrapped version of Mack's model which allows to compute a predictive distribution. In the interest to be concise, we will not discuss more about this model, and we invite the reader to take a look at Mack (1993) and England and Verrall (2002) for more details.

In the collective GLM framework, we assume that the incremental aggregate payments Y_{ij} are independent and follow a distribution falling into the exponential family with expected value given by $g\left(E[Y_{ij}]\right) = \beta_0 + \alpha_i + \beta_j$, where $g()$ is the link function, α_i, $i = 2, 3, \ldots, N$ is the accident year effect, β_j, $j = 2, 3, \ldots, N$ is the development year effect and β_0 is the intercept. Variance is given by $\text{Var}[Y_{ij}] = \varphi V\left(E[Y_{ij}]\right)$, where $V()$ is the variance function and φ is the dispersion parameter (see De Jong and Heller (2008) for an introduction to GLM). The prediction for Y_{ij} is then given by

$$\widehat{Y}_{ij} = g^{-1}(\widehat{\beta}_0 + \widehat{\alpha}_i + \widehat{\beta}_j),$$

where estimates of the parameters $\widehat{\beta}_0$, $\{\widehat{\alpha}_i\}_{i=2}^N$ and $\{\widehat{\beta}_j\}_{j=2}^N$ are usually found by maximizing likelihood. The reserve at time t^* can thereafter be computed using Equation (1), and the predictive distribution of the total reserve can be calculated using simulations. A complete description of this model is done in Wüthrich and Merz (2008).

The individual GLM for loss reserving which we present here represents a micro-level version of the collective GLM described in the last paragraph. A major advantage of this model over the collective version comes from the use of covariates in addition to the accident and development year. Adaptations, minor or not, of our chosen approach could be studied as well, but this is not the main purpose of this paper. We assume that $Y_j^{(k)}$ follows a distribution falling into the exponential family with expected value given by $g\left(E\left[Y_j^{(k)}\right]\right) = x_j^{(k)}\beta$ and variance given by $\text{Var}\left[Y_j^{(k)}\right] = \varphi V\left(E\left[Y_j^{(k)}\right]\right)$, where $x_j^{(k)}$ is the vector of covariates for claim k and development period j and β is the usual vector of parameters. The prediction for $Y_j^{(k)}$ is obtained with

$$\widehat{Y}_j^{(k)} = g^{-1}\left(x_j^{(k)}\widehat{\beta}\right),$$

where $\widehat{\beta}$ is the maximum likelihood estimator of β. For a claim from occurrence period i in the portfolio, the individual reserve, evaluated at t^*, is given by $\widehat{R}_{t^*}^{(k)} = \sum_{j=I+2-i}^{I} \widehat{Y}_j^{(k)}$, and the total RBNS reserve is given by $\widehat{R}_{t^*} = \sum_k \widehat{R}_{t^*}^{(k)}$. Some remarks should be made concerning the implementation of this model. First, the distribution of the random variable $Y_j^{(k)}$ has a mass at 0 because we did not separate occurrence and severity in our modeling. It may also be possible to consider a two-part GLM. Secondly, this model assumes that the covariates remain identical after the valuation date, which is not exactly accurate in the presence of dynamic variables such as the number of healthcare providers. We discuss this issue in more detail in the next subsection. Third, the status of a file (open or closed) is used as an explanatory variable in the model, which implicitly allows for reopening. Finally, obtaining the IBNR reserve also requires a model for the occurrence of a claim and the delay of its declaration to the insurer in addition to more assumptions about the composition of the portfolio.

3.2. Gradient Boosting for Loss Reserving

In order to train gradient boosting models, we use an algorithm called XGBoost developed by Chen and Guestrin (2016), and regression trees are chosen as weak learners. For more detail about XGBoost algorithm and regression trees, see Breiman et al. (1984); Chen and Guestrin (2016), respectively. The loss function used is the squared loss $L(y, f(x)) = (y - f(x))^2$ but other options such as residual deviance for gamma regression were considered without significantly altering the conclusions. A more detailed analysis of the impact of the choice of this function is deferred to a subsequent case study. Models were built using R programming language in conjunction with caret and xgboost libraries. caret is a powerful package used to train and to validate a wide range of statistical models including XGBoost algorithm.

Let us say we have a portfolio $\mathcal{S}$ on which we want to train an XGBoost model for loss reserving. This portfolio contains both, open and closed claims. At this stage, several options are available:

1. The simplest solution is to train the model on data $\mathcal{D}_T$ where only settled claims (or non-censored claims) are included. Hence, the response is known for all claims. However, this leads to a selection bias because claims that are already settled at t^* tend to have shorter developments, and claims with shorter development tend to have lower total paid amounts. Consequently, the model is almost exclusively trained on simple claims with low training responses, which leads to underestimation of the total paid amounts for new claims. Furthermore, a significant proportion of the claims are removed from the analysis, which causes a loss of information. We will analyze this bias further in Section 4 (see model B).
2. In Lopez et al. (2016), a different and interesting approach is proposed: in order to correct the selection bias induced by the presence of censored data, a strategy called "inverse probability of censoring weighting" (IPCW) is implemented, which involves assigning weights to observations to offset the lack of complete observations in the sample. The weights are determined using the Kaplan-Meier estimator of the censoring distribution, and a modified CART algorithm is used to make the predictions.
3. A third approach is to develop claims that are still open at t^* using parameters from a classical approach such as Mack's or the GLM model. We discuss this idea in more detail in Section 4 (see model C and model D).

In order to predict total paid amount for a claim k, we use information we have about the case at evaluation date t^*, denoted by $x_{t^*}^{(k)}$.

Some of the covariates, such as the accident year, are static, which means their value do not change over time. These covariates are quite easy to handle because their final value is known since the reporting of the claims. However, some of the available information is expected to develop between t^* and the closure date, for example, the claimant's health status or the number of healthcare providers in the file. To handle those dynamic covariates, we have, at least, the following two options:

- we can assume that they are static, which can lead to a bias in the predictions obtained (see model E in Section 4); or
- we can, for each of these variables, (1) adjust a dynamic model, (2) obtain a prediction of the complete trajectory, and (3) use the algorithm conditionally to the realization of this trajectory. Moreover, there may be dependence between these variables, which would warrant a multivariate approach.

These two points will be discussed in Section 4 (see model E). The XGBoost algorithm therefore learns a prediction function $\hat{f}_{XGB}$ on the adjusted dataset, depending on the selected option 1., 2. or 3. and how dynamic covariates are handled. Then, the predicted total paid amount for claim k is given by $\widehat{C}_{T_3}^{(k)} = \hat{f}_{XGB}\left(x_{t^*}^{(k)}\right)$. Reserve for claim k is $\widehat{R}_{t^*}^{(k)} = \widehat{C}_{T_3}^{(k)} - C_{t^*}^{(k)}$, and the RBNS reserve for the whole portfolio is computed with $\widehat{R}_{t^*} = \sum_{k \in \mathcal{S}} \widehat{R}_{t^*}^{(k)}$. Gradient boosting is a non-parametric algorithm and no distribution is assumed for the response variable. Therefore, in order to compute the variance of the reserve and some risk measures, we use a non-parametric bootstrap procedure.

4. Analyses

In this section, we present an extended case study based on a detailed dataset from a property and casualty insurance company. In Section 4.1, we describe the dataset, in Section 4.2 we explain how we construct and train our models, and in Section 4.4 we present our numerical results and analyses.

4.1. Data

We analyzed a North American database consisting of 67.203 claims occurred from 1 Januar 2004 to 31 December 2016. We therefore let τ, the starting point, be 1 January 2004 meaning that all dates are expressed in number of years from this date. These claims are related to 60.075 general liability insurance policies for private individuals. We focus only on the accident benefits coverage that provides compensation if the insured is injured or killed in an auto accident. It also includes coverage for passengers and pedestrians involved in the accident. Claims involve one (83%), two (13%) or 3+ parties (4%) resulting in a total of 82.520 files in the database. Consequently, there is a possibility of dependence between some payments in the database. Nevertheless, we assume in this paper that all files are independent claims, and we postpone the analysis of this dependence. Thus, we analyze a portfolio of 82.520 independent claims that we denote by $\mathcal{S}$. An example of the structure of the dataset is given in Table A1 in Appendix A.

The data are longitudinal, and each row of the database corresponds to a snapshot of a file. For each element in $\mathcal{S}$, a snapshot is taken at the end of every quarter, and we have information from the reporting date until 31 December 2016. Therefore, a claim is represented by a maximum of 52 rows. A line is added in the database even if there is no new information, i.e., it could be possible that two consecutive lines provide precisely the same information. During the training of our models, we do not consider these replicate rows because they do not provide any relevant information for the model.

The information vector for claim k, $k = 1, \ldots, 82.520$ at time t is given by $\mathcal{D}_t^{(k)} = (x_t^{(k)}, C_t^{(k)})$. Therefore, the information matrix about the whole portfolio at time t is given by $\mathcal{D}_t^{(\mathcal{S})} = \{\mathcal{D}_t^{(k)}\}_{k \in \mathcal{S}}$. Because of the discrete nature of our dataset, it contains information $\{\mathcal{D}_t^{(\mathcal{S})}\}_{\{0.25t:\, t \in \mathbb{N},\, t \leq 52\}}$, where t is the number of years since τ.

In order to validate models, we need to know how much has actually been paid for each claim. In portfolio $\mathcal{S}$, the total paid amount C_{T_3} is still unknown for 19% of the cases because they are related to claims that were open on 31 December 2016 (see Figure 2). To overcome this issue, we use a subset $\mathcal{S}_7 = \{k \in \mathcal{S} : T_1^{(k)} < 7\}$ of $\mathcal{S}$, i.e., we consider only accident years from 2004 to 2010 for both training and validation. This subset contains 36.286 files related to 32.260 claims of which 22% are still open on 31 December 2010. Further, only 0.67% of the files are associated with claims that are still open as of the end of 2016, so we know the exact total paid amount for 99.33% of them, assuming no reopening after 2016. For the small proportion of open claims, we assume that the incurred amount set by experts is the true total paid amount. Hence, the evaluation date is set at 31 December 2010 and $t^* = 7$. This is the date at which the reserve must be evaluated for files in $\mathcal{S}_7$. This implies that the models are not allowed to use information past this date for their training. Information past the evaluation date is used only for validation.

For simplicity and for computational purposes, the quarterly database is summarized to form a yearly database $\{\mathcal{D}_t^{(\mathcal{S}_7)}\}_{t=1}^{13}$, where $\mathcal{D}_t^{(\mathcal{S}_7)} = \{\mathcal{D}_t^{(k)}\}_{k \in \mathcal{S}_7}$. We randomly sampled 70% of the 36.843 claims to form the training set of indices $\mathcal{T} \subset \mathcal{S}_7$, and the other 30% forms the validation set of indices $\mathcal{V} \subset \mathcal{S}_7$, which gives the training and validation datasets $\mathcal{D}_\mathcal{T} = \{\mathcal{D}_t^{(\mathcal{T})}\}_{t=1}^{13}$ and $\mathcal{D}_\mathcal{V} = \{\mathcal{D}_t^{(\mathcal{V})}\}_{t=1}^{13}$.

In partnership with the insurance company, we selected 20 covariates in order to predict total paid amount for each of the claims. To make all models comparable, we use the same covariates for all claims. Some covariates are characteristics of the insured, such as age and gender, and some pertain to the claim such as the accident year, the development year, and the number of healthcare providers in the file. For privacy reasons, we cannot discuss the selected covariates further in this paper.

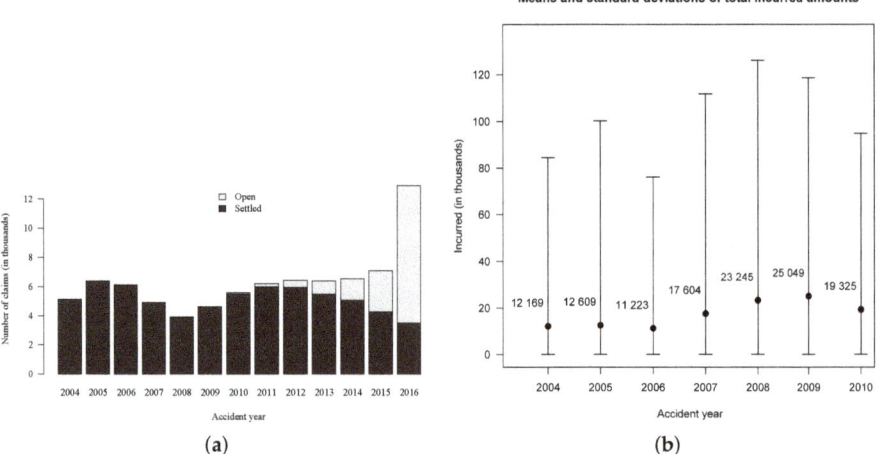

Figure 2. (a) Status of claims of incurred amounts on 31 December 2016; (b) Means and standard deviations of incurred amounts on 31 December 2016.

4.2. Training of XGBoost Models

In order to train XGBoost models, we analyze the training dataset $\mathcal{D}_\mathcal{T} = \{(x_t, C_t)\}_{t=1}^{13}$. Because some covariates are dynamic, the design matrix x_t changes over time, that is to say $x_t \neq x_{t'}$ for $t \neq t'$. Unless otherwise stated, the models are all trained using x_7, which is the latest information we have about files, assuming information after $t^* = 7$ is unknown.

Although a model using real responses is not usable in practice, it is possible to train it because we set the evaluation date to be in the past. Model A acts as a benchmark model in our case study because it is fit using C_{T_3} as training responses and it is best model we can hope for. Therefore, in order to train model A, data $\mathcal{D}_\mathcal{T}^A = \{(x_7^{(k)}, C_{T_3}^{(k)})\}_{k \in \mathcal{T}}$ is input into the XGBoost algorithm, which learns the prediction function $\widehat{f}_A$.

Model B, which is biased, is fit using C_7 as training responses, but only on the set of claims for which the claim is settled at time $t^* = 7$. Hence, model B is trained using $\mathcal{D}_\mathcal{T}^B = \{(x_7^{(k)}, C_7^{(k)})\}_{k \in \mathcal{T}_B}$, where $\mathcal{T}_B = \{k \in \mathcal{T} : T_3^{(k)} < 7\}$, giving the prediction function $\widehat{f}_B$. This model allows us to measure the extent of the selection bias.

In the next models, we develop claims that are still open at t^*, i.e., we predict pseudo-responses $\widehat{C}_{T_3}$ using training set $\mathcal{D}_\mathcal{T}$, and these $\widehat{C}_{T_3}$ are subsequently used to fit the model.

In model C, claims are developed using the Mack's model. We only develop open files at the evaluation date, i.e., we assume no reopening for settled claims. More specifically, information from data $\{\mathcal{D}_t^{(\mathcal{T})}\}_{t=1}^7$ is aggregated by accident year and by development year to form a cumulative run-off triangle. Based on this triangle, we use the bootstrap approach described in England and Verrall (2002) and involving Pearson's residuals to generate $B = 1000$ bootstrapped triangles $\{C^{(b)}\}_{b=1}^B$. On each of those triangles, the Mack's model is applied to obtain vectors of development factors $\widehat{\lambda}_j = \{\lambda_j^{(b)}\}_{b=1}^B$, $j = 1, \ldots, 6$, with

$$\widehat{\lambda}_j^{(b)} = \frac{\sum_{i=1}^{7-j} C_{i(j+1)}^{(b)}}{\sum_{i=1}^{7-j} C_{ij}^{(b)}}, \quad b = 1, \ldots, B, \tag{3}$$

where $C^{(b)}_{i(j+1)}$ and $C^{(b)}_{ij}$ are from bootstrapped triangle $C^{(b)}$. From each vector $\hat{\lambda}_j$, we compute empirical cumulative distribution function F_j and we set $\hat{\lambda}_j = F_j^{-1}(\kappa_C)$, $j = 1, \ldots, 6$ and where κ_C is a hyperparameter estimated using cross-validation. Finally, we calculate pseudo-responses $\{\hat{C}^{(k)}_{T_3}\}_{k \in \mathcal{T}}$ using

$$\hat{C}^{(k)}_{T_3} = \hat{\lambda}^c_j C^{(k)}_7, \text{ where } \hat{\lambda}^c_j = \prod_{l=j}^{6} \hat{\lambda}_l. \tag{4}$$

In model D, claims are projected using an individual quasi-Poisson GLM as described in Section 3.1 and including all 20 covariates. We discretize the amounts by rounding in order to be able to use a counting distribution even if the response variable is theoretically continuous. This approach is common in the literature associated with loss reserving and does not have a significant impact on the final results. Unlike in model C, we also develop settled claims at $t^* = 7$. This is because in this model, the status (open or closed) of the file is used, which means the models will be able to make the difference between open and settled claims. More specifically, model D uses an individual quasi-Poisson GLM to estimate the training dependent variable. The GLM is fit on data $\{(x_t^{(\mathcal{T})}, Y_t^{(\mathcal{T})})\}_{t=1}^{7}$, where $x_t^{(\mathcal{T})} = \{x_t^{(k)}\}_{k \in \mathcal{T}}$, $Y_t^{(\mathcal{T})} = \{Y_t^{(k)}\}_{k \in \mathcal{T}}$ and $Y_t^{(k)}$ is the yearly aggregate payment at year t for claim k. A logarithm link function is used and coefficients are estimated by maximizing the Poisson log-likelihood function. Therefore, the estimation of the expected value for a new observation is given by

$$\hat{\mu}_t^{(k)} = \exp\left(x_t^{(k)} \hat{\beta}\right),$$

and a prediction is made according to $\hat{Y}_t^{(k)} = F^{-1}_{Y_t^{(k)}}(\kappa_D)$, which is the level κ_D empirical quantile of the distribution of $Y_t^{(k)}$. This quantile can be obtained using simulation or bootstrap procedure. Finally, for the claim k, the pseudo-response is

$$\hat{C}^{(k)}_{T_3} = C_7^{(k)} + \sum_{t=8}^{13} \hat{Y}_t^{(k)}.$$

Model E is constructed in the same way as model C but it uses prospective information about the 4 dynamic stochastic covariates available in the dataset. It is analogous to model A in the sense that it is not usable in practice. However, fitting this model indicates whether an additional model that would project censored dynamic covariates would be useful. In Table 1, we summarize the main specifications of the models.

Table 1. Main specifications of XGBoost models.

Model	Response Variable ($\hat{C}_{T_3}$)	Covariates	Usable in Practice?
Model A	$\{C_{T_3}\}$	x_7	No
Model B	$\{C_7^{(k)}\}_{k \in \mathcal{T}_B}$, $\mathcal{T}_B = \{k \in \mathcal{T} : T_3^{(k)} < 7\}$	x_7	Yes
Model C	closed: $\{C_7\}$ open: $\{\hat{\lambda}^c_j C_7\}$ ($\hat{\lambda}$ from bootstrap)	x_7 x_7	Yes
Model D	all: $\{C_7 + \sum_{t=8}^{13} \hat{Y}_t\}$ (with $\hat{Y}_t = q_{Y_t}(\kappa_D)$)	x_7	Yes
Model E	closed: $\{C_7\}$ open: $\{\hat{\lambda}^c_j C_7\}$ ($\hat{\lambda}$ from bootstrap)	x_{13} x_{13}	No

Note: unless otherwise stated, we have $k \in \mathcal{T}$.

4.3. Learning of Prediction Function

In Section 4.2, we showed how to train the XGBoost models having the dataset $\mathcal{D}_\mathcal{T}$. However, no details were given on how we obtain the prediction function for each model. In this section, we dive one abstraction level lower by explaining the general idea behind the algorithm. Our presentation is closely inspired by the TreeBoost algorithm developed by Friedman (2001), which is based on the same principles as XGBoost using regression trees as weak learners. The main difference between the two algorithms is the computation time: XGBoost is usually faster to train. In order to get through this, we take model A as an example. The explanation is nevertheless easily transferable to all other models since only the dataset given as input changes.

In the regression framework, a TreeBoost algorithm combines many regression trees together in order to optimize some objective function and thus learn a prediction function. The prediction function for model A takes the form of a weighted sum of regression tress

$$\hat{f}_A\left(x_7^{(k)}\right) = \sum_{m=1}^{M} \beta_m T\left(x_7^{(k)}; \theta_m\right), \quad (5)$$

where $\{\beta_m\}_{m=1}^{M}$ and $\{\theta_m\}_{m=1}^{M}$ are the weights and the vectors of parameters characterizing the regression trees, respectively. The vector of parameters associated with the mth tree contains J_m regions (or leaves) $\{R_{jm}\}_{j=1}^{J_m}$ as well as the corresponding prediction constants $\{\gamma_{jm}\}_{j=1}^{J_m}$, which means $\theta_m = \{R_{jm}, \gamma_{jm}\}_{j=1}^{J_m}$. Notice that a regression tree can be seen as a weighted sum of indicator functions:

$$T(x; \theta) = \sum_{j=1}^{J} \gamma_j \mathbb{1}(x \in R_j).$$

Ref. Friedman (2001) proposed to slightly modify Equation (5) in order to choose a different optimal value β_{jm} for each of the tree's regions. Consequently, each weight β_{jm} can be absorbed into the prediction constant γ_{jm}. Assuming a constant number of regions J in each tree (which is almost always the case in practice), Equation (5) becomes

$$\hat{f}_A\left(x_7^{(k)}\right) = \sum_{m=1}^{M} \sum_{j=1}^{J} \gamma_{jm} \mathbb{1}\left(x_7^{(k)} \in R_{jm}\right).$$

With a loss function $\mathcal{L}()$, we need to solve

$$\{\beta_m, \theta_m\}_{m=1}^{M} = \arg\min_{\{\beta'_m, \theta'_m\}} \sum_{k \in \mathcal{T}} \mathcal{L}\left(C_{T_3}^{(k)}, \sum_{m=1}^{M} \sum_{j=1}^{J} \gamma_{jm} \mathbb{1}\left(x_7^{(k)} \in R_{jm}\right)\right),$$

which is, most of the time, too expensive computationally. The TreeBoost algorithm overcomes this issue by building the prediction function iteratively. In order to avoid overfitting, it also adds a learning rate ν, $0 < \nu \leq 1$. The steps needed to obtain the prediction function for model A are detailed in Algorithm 1.

Algorithm 1: Obtaining $\widehat{f}_A$ with least square TreeBoost.

Input: data $\mathcal{D}_{\mathcal{T}}^A = \left\{\left(x_7^{(k)}, C_{T_3}^{(k)}\right)\right\}_{k \in \mathcal{T}}$, number of trees M, number of regions in each tree J, learning rate ν

Initialize: $f_A^{(0)}\left(x_7^{(k)}\right) := \underset{k \in \mathcal{T}}{\text{average}} \left\{C_{T_3}^{(k)}\right\}$

for $m \leftarrow 1$ **to** M **do**
- compute residuals of the current model

$$r_m^{(k)} := C_{T_3}^{(k)} - f_A^{(m-1)}\left(x_7^{(k)}\right), \quad \text{for } k \in \mathcal{T};$$

- fit a tree to the data $\left\{\left(x_7^{(k)}, r_m^{(k)}\right)\right\}_{k \in \mathcal{T}}$, yielding regions $\{R_{jm}\}_{j=1}^J$;
- compute prediction constant for each region

$$\gamma_{jm} = \underset{\left\{k : x_7^{(k)} \in R_{jm}\right\}}{\text{average}} \left\{r_m^{(k)}\right\}, \quad \text{for } j = 1, \ldots, J;$$

- update the model

$$f_A^{(m)}\left(x_7^{(k)}\right) := f_A^{(m-1)}\left(x_7^{(k)}\right) + \nu \sum_{j=1}^{J} \gamma_{jm} \mathbb{1}\left(x_7^{(k)} \in R_{jm}\right);$$

end
return $\widehat{f}_A := f_A^{(M)}$

4.4. Results

From $\{\mathcal{D}_t^{(\mathcal{T})}\}_{t=1}^7$, which was the training dataset before the evaluation date, it is possible to obtain a training run-off triangle by aggregating payments by accident and by development year, presented in Table 2.

Table 2. Training incremental run-off triangle (in \$100,000).

Development Year	1	2	3	4	5	6	7
Accident year							
2004	79	102	66	49	57	48	37
2005	83	128	84	55	52	41	·
2006	91	138	69	49	38	·	·
2007	111	155	98	61	·	·	·
2008	100	178	99	·	·	·	·
2009	137	251	·	·	·	·	·
2010	155	·	·	·	·	·	·

We can apply the same principle for validation dataset $\mathcal{D}_\mathcal{V}$, which yields the validation run-off triangle displayed in Table 3.

Table 3. Validation incremental run-off triangle (in $100,000).

Development Year	1	2	3	4	5	6	7	8+
Accident year								
2004	34	41	23	13	14	14	9	7
2005	37	60	36	29	45	21	20	24
2006	41	64	34	23	21	14	4	21
2007	46	67	40	37	15	18	3	13
2008	46	82	39	42	16	11	15	33
2009	54	109	62	51	31	36	11	2
2010	66	93	47	45	16	16	9	?

Note: Data used to score models are displayed in black as aggregated payments used for validation are in gray.

Based on the training run-off triangle, it is possible to fit many collective models, see Wüthrich and Merz (2008) for an extensive overview. Once fitted, we scored them on the validation triangle. In the validation triangle (Table 3), data used to score models are displayed in black and aggregated payments observed after the evaluation date are displayed in gray. Payments have been observed for six years after 2010, but this was not long enough for all claims to be settled. In fact, on 31 December 2016, 0.67% of files were associated with claims that are still open, mostly from accident years 2009 and 2010. Therefore, amounts in column "8+" for accident years 2009 and 2010 in Table 3 are in fact too low. Based on available information, the observed RBNS amount was $67,619,905 (summing all gray entries), but we can reasonably think that this amount would be closer to $70,000,000 if we could observe more years. The observed IBNR amount was $3,625,983 for a total amount of $71,245,888.

Results for collective models are presented according to two approaches:

- Mack's model, for which we present results obtained with the bootstrap approach developed by England and Verrall (2002), based on both quasi-Poisson and gamma distributions; and
- generalized linear models for which we present results obtained using a logarithmic link function and a variance function $\mathcal{V}(\mu) = \phi\mu^p$ with $p = 1$ (quasi-Poisson), $p = 2$ (gamma), and $1 < p < 2$ (Tweedie).

For each model, Table 4 presents the expected value of the reserve, its standard error, and the 95% and the 99% quantiles of the predictive distribution of the total reserve amount. As is generally the case, the choice of the distribution used to simulate the process error in the bootstrap procedure for Mack's model has no significant impact on the results. Reasonable practices, at least in North America, generally require a reserve amount given by a high quantile (95%, 99% or even 99.5%) of the reserve's predictive distribution. As a result, the reserve amount obtained by bootstrapping Mack's model is too high (between $90,000,000 and $100,000,000) compared to the observed value (approximately $70,000,000). Reserve amounts obtained with generalized linear models were more reasonable (between $77,000,000 and $83,000,000), regardless of the choice of the underlying distribution. The predictive distribution for all collective models is shown in Figure 3.

In Table 4, we also present in-sample results, i.e., we used the same dataset to perform both estimation and validation. The results were very similar, which tends to indicate stability of the results obtained using these collective approaches.

Individual models were trained on the training set $\{\mathcal{D}_t^{(T)}\}_{t=1}^{7}$ and scored on the validation set $\{\mathcal{D}^{(V)}\}_{t=8}^{13}$. In contrast to collective approaches, individual methods used micro-covariates and, more specifically, the reporting date. This allows us to distinguish between IBNR claims and RBNS claims and, as previously mentioned, in this project we mainly focus on the modeling of the RBNS reserve. Nevertheless, in our dataset, we observe very few IBNR claims ($3,625,983) and therefore, we can reasonably compare the results obtained using both micro- and macro-level models with the observed amount ($67,619,905).

Table 4. Prediction results (incurred but not reported (IBNR) + reported but not settled (RBNS)) for collective approaches.

Model	Assessment	E[Res.]	$\sqrt{\text{Var[Res.]}}$	$q_{0.95}$	$q_{0.99}$
Bootstrap Mack	out-of-sample	76,795,136	7,080,826	89,086,213	95,063,184
(quasi-Poisson)	in-sample	75,019,768	8,830,631	90,242,398	97,954,554
Bootstrap Mack	out-of-sample	76,803,753	7,170,529	89,133,141	95,269,308
(Gamma)	in-sample	75,004,053	8,842,412	90,500,323	98,371,607
GLM	out-of-sample	75,706,046	2,969,877	80,655,890	82,696,002
(Quasi-Poisson)	in-sample	74,778,091	3,084,216	79,922,183	81,996,425
GLM	out-of-sample	73,518,411	2,263,714	77,276,416	78,907,812
(Gamma)	in-sample	71,277,218	3,595,958	77,343,035	80,204,504
GLM	out-of-sample	75,688,916	2,205,003	79,317,520	80,871,729
(Tweedie)	in-sample	74,706,050	2,197,659	78,260,722	79,790,056

Note: because 70% of the data was used for training and 30% is used for testing, we used a factor of 7/3 to correct in-sample predictions and make them comparable with out-of-sample predictions. The observed total amount was $71,245,888.

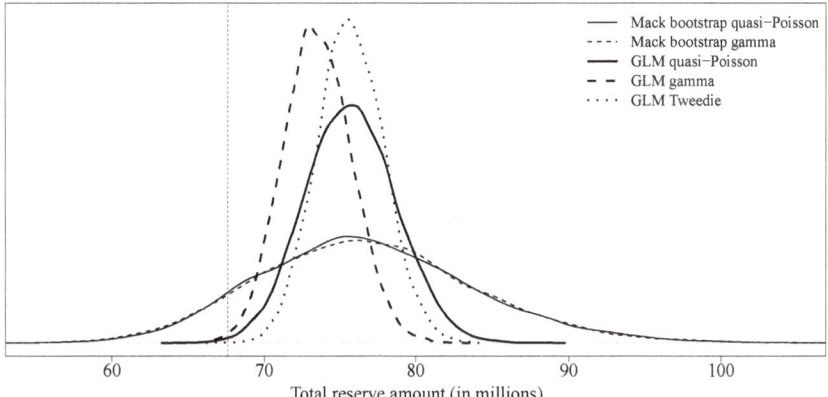

Figure 3. Comparison of predictive distributions (incurred but not reported (IBNR) + reported but not settled (RBNS)) for collective models.

We considered the following approaches:

- individual generalized linear models (see Section 3.1), for which we present results obtained using a logarithmic link function and three variance functions: $\mathcal{V}(\mu) = \mu$ (Poisson) and $\mathcal{V}(\mu) = \phi \mu^p$ with $p = 1$ (quasi-Poisson) and $\mathcal{V}(\mu) = \phi \mu^p$ with $1 < p < 2$ (Tweedie); and
- XGBoost models (models A, B, C, D and E) described in Section 4.2.

Both approaches used the same covariates described in Section 4.1, which makes them comparable. For many files in both training and validation sets, some covariates are missing. Because generalized linear models cannot handle missing values, median/mode imputation has been performed for both training and validation sets. No imputation has been done for XGBoost models because missing values are processed automatically by the algorithm.

Results for individual GLM are displayed in Table 5, and predictive distributions for both quasi-Poisson and Tweedie GLM are shown in Figure 4. Predictive distribution for the Poisson GLM is omitted because it is the same as the quasi-Poisson model, but with a much smaller variance. Based on our dataset, we observe that the estimated value of the parameter associated to some covariates is particularly dependent on the database used to train the model, e.g., in the worst case, for the quasi-Poisson model, we observe $\hat{\beta} = 0.169$ (0.091) with the out-of-sample approach and $\hat{\beta} = -1.009$ (0.154) with the in-sample approach. This can also be observed for many parameters of the model, as shown in Figure 5 for the quasi-Poisson model. These results were obtained by resampling from the training database and the quasi-Poisson model. Crosses and circles represent the estimated values of the parameters if the original training database is used, and the estimated values of the parameters if the validation database is used, respectively. On this graph, we observe that, for most of the parameters, the values estimated on the validation set are inaccessible when the model is adjusted on the training set. In Table 5, we display results for both in-sample and out-of-sample approaches. As the results shown in Figure 4 suggest, there are significant differences between the two approaches. Particularly, the reserves obtained from the out-of-sample approach are too high compared with the observed value. Although it is true that in practice, the training/validation set division is less relevant for an individual generalized linear model because the risk of overfitting is lower, this suggests that some caution is required in a context of loss reserving.

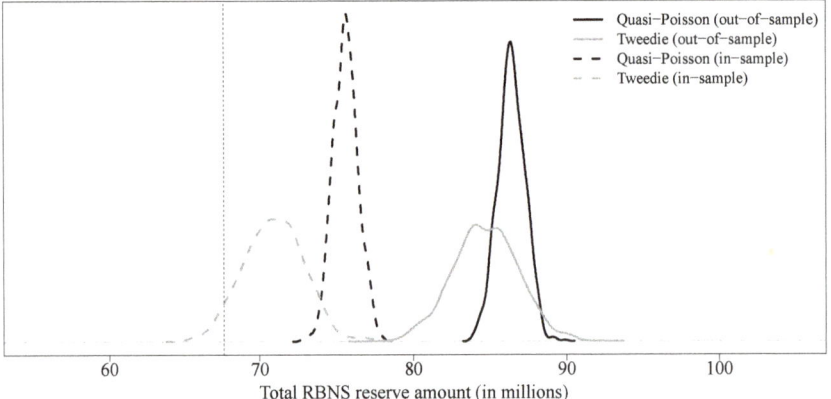

Figure 4. Predictive distributions (RBNS) for individual GLM with covariates.

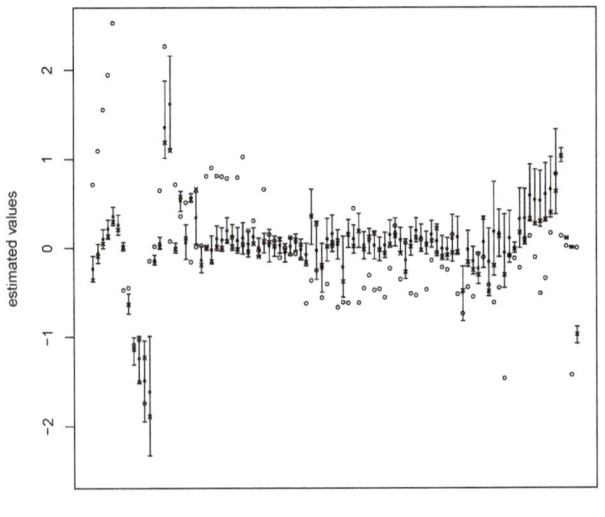

Figure 5. Means and 95% confidence intervals for all parameters of the model.

Table 5. Prediction results (RBNS) for individual generalized linear models using covariates.

Model	Assessment	E[Res.]	$\sqrt{\text{Var[Res.]}}$	$q_{0.95}$	$q_{0.99}$
Poisson	out-of-sample	86,411,734	9007	86,426,520	86,431,211
	in-sample	75,611,203	8655	75,625,348	75,631,190
Quasi-Poisson	out-of-sample	86,379,296	894,853	87,815,685	88,309,697
	in-sample	75,606,230	814,608	76,984,768	77,433,248
Tweedie	out-of-sample	84,693,529	2,119,280	88,135,187	90,011,542
	in-sample	70,906,225	1,994,004	74,098,686	75,851,991

Note: Because 70% of the data is used for training and 30% is used for testing, we use a factor of 7/3 to correct in-sample predictions and make them comparable with out-of-sample predictions. The observed RBNS amount is $67,619,905.

Out-of-sample results for XGBoost models are displayed in Table 6. For all models, the learning rate is around 10%, which means our models are quite robust to overfitting. We use a maximum depth of 3 for each tree. A higher value would make our model more complex but also less robust to overfitting. All those hyperparameters are obtained by cross-validation. Parameters $\kappa_C = 0.8$ and $\kappa_D = 0.8$ are obtained using cross-validation over a grid given by $\{0.6, 0.7, 0.8, 0.9\}$.

Table 6. Prediction results (RBNS) for individual approaches (XGBoost) using covariates.

Model	E[Res.]	$\sqrt{\text{Var[Res.]}}$	$q_{0.95}$	$q_{0.99}$
Model A	73,204,299	3,742,971	79,329,916	82,453,032
Model B	14,339,470	6,723,608	25,757,061	30,643,369
Model C	67,655,960	2,411,739	71,708,313	73,762,242
Model D	68,313,731	4,176,418	75,408,868	78,517,966
Model E	67,772,822	2,387,476	71,722,744	73,540,516

Note: The observed RBNS amount is $67,619,905.

Not surprisingly, we observe that model B is completely off the mark, underestimating the total reserve by a large amount. This confirms that the selection bias, at least in this example, is real and substantial.

model C considers a collective model, i.e., without micro-covariates, to create pseudo-responses and uses all covariates available in order to predict final paid amounts. With a slightly lower expectation and variance, model C is quite similar to model A. Because the latter model uses real responses for its training, the method used for claim development appears to be reasonable. Model D uses an individual model, a quasi-Poisson GLM, using all covariates available to obtain both, pseudo-responses and final predictions. Again, results are similar to those of model A. In Figure 6 we compare the predictive distributions of model A, model C and model D.

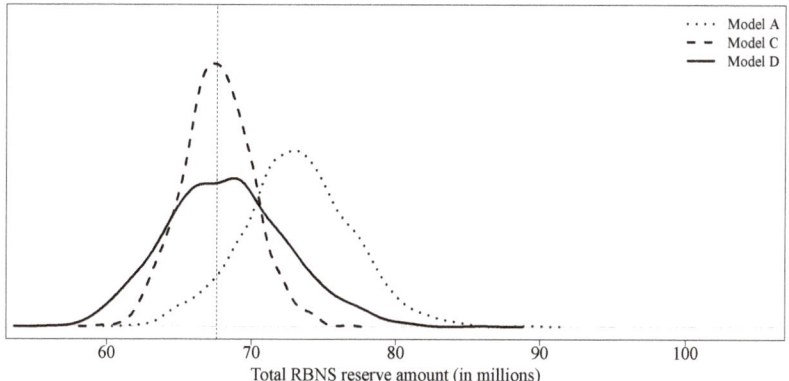

Figure 6. Predictive distributions (RBNS) for XGBoost models A, C and D.

Model E is identical to model C with the exception of dynamic variables whose value at the evaluation date was artificially replaced by the ultimate value. At least in this case study, the impact is negligible (see Figure 7). There would be no real interest in building a hierarchical model that allows, first, to develop the dynamic variables and, second, to use one XGBoost models to predict final paid amounts.

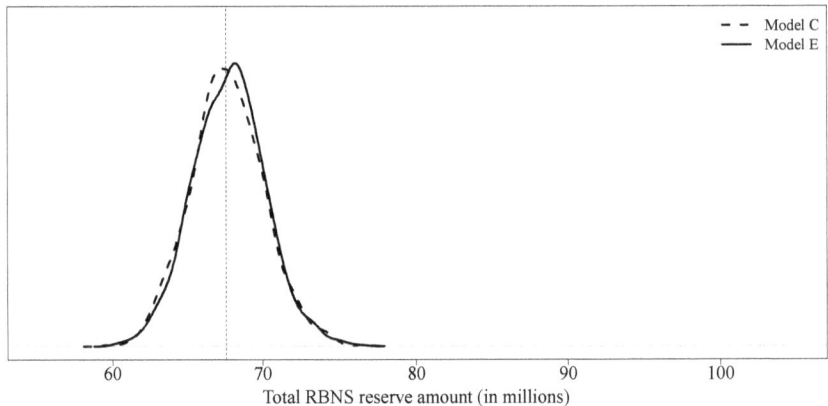

Figure 7. Comparison of predictive distributions for models E and C.

5. Conclusions

This paper studies the modeling of loss reserves for a property and casualty insurance company using micro-level approaches. More specifically, we apply generalized linear models and gradient boosting models designed to take into account the characteristics of each individual policyholder, as well as individual claims. We compare those models to classical approaches and show their performance on a detailed dataset from a Canadian insurance company. The choice of a gradient boosted decision-tree model is motivated by its strong performance for prediction on structured data. In addition, this type of algorithm requires very little data preprocessing, which is a notable benefit. The XGBoost algorithm was chosen for this analysis, mainly for its relatively short calculation time.

Through a case study, we mainly showed that

(1) the censored nature of the data could strongly bias the loss reserving process; and
(2) the use of a micro-level model based solely on generalized linear models could be unstable for loss reserving but an approach combining a macro-level (or a micro-level) model for the artificial completion of open claims and a micro-level gradient-boosting model represents an interesting approach for an insurance company.

The gradient boosting models presented in this paper allow insurers to compute a prediction for the total paid amount of each claim. Insurers might also be interested in modeling the payment schedule, namely to predict the date and the amount of each individual payment. Moreover, we know that payments for parties belonging to the same claim are not independent and are positively correlated. Therefore, one could extend the model by adding a dependence structure between parties. The same principle could be applied with the different types of coverage (medical and rehabilitation, income replacement, etc.). Dynamic covariates can change over time, which makes their future value random. In this work, we assumed that their value will not change after the evaluation date and we checked that the impact was not very high. However, for a different database, this could have a significant impact on the results. A possible refinement would be to build a hierarchical model that first predicts the ultimate values of dynamic covariates before inputting them in the gradient boosting algorithm.

In recent years, several new individual approaches have been proposed. It will be interesting, in a future case study, to compare the results obtained, on the same database, using these different methods. Finally, in this case study, we always consider predictive distributions to compare models. One might wonder why we do not use criteria often used in machine learning such as the root mean squared error (RMSE) or the mean absolute error (MAE). The reason lies, at least in part, in the fact that the database used in this work contains numerous small (or zero) claims and very few large claims. Therefore, because RMSE and MAE are symmetric error functions, they favor models that predict low reserves. Expectile regression is an avenue that is being explored to overcome this weakness.

Author Contributions: Both authors contributed equally to this work.

Funding: We acknowledge the support of the Natural Sciences and Engineering Research Council of Canada (NSERC).

Acknowledgments: We thank three anonymous referees who have substantially helped to improve the paper through their constructive comments. We also thank our industrial partner for the database.

Conflicts of Interest: The authors declare no conflict of interest.

Appendix A. Structure of the Dataset

Table A1. An example of the structure of the database.

Policy Number	Claim Number	Party	File Number	Date	...
P100000	C234534	1	F0000001	31 March 2004	...
P100000	C234534	1	F0000001	30 June 2004	...
P100000	C234534	1	F0000001	30 September 2004	...
...	...	...	...	...	...
P100000	C234534	2	F0000002	31 March 2004	...
P100000	C234534	2	F0000002	30 June 2004	...
P100000	C234534	2	F0000002	30 September 2004	...
...	...	...	...	...	...
P100034	C563454	1	F0000140	31 March 2004	...
P100034	C563454	1	F0000140	30 June 2004	...
P100034	C563454	1	F0000140	30 September 2004	...
...	...	...	...	...	...

Note: It can be seen that the contract P100000 generated a claim involving two people, i.e., the driver and a passenger, and generating two files. In our analysis, files F0000001 and F0000002 are considered to be independent claims. A snapshot of the available information is taken at the end of each quarter.

References

Antonio, Katrien, and Richard Plat. 2014. Micro-level stochastic loss reserving for general insurance. *Scandinavian Actuarial Journal* 7: 649–69. [CrossRef]

Arjas, Elja. 1989. The claims reserving problem in non-life insurance: Some structural ideas. *ASTIN Bulletin* 19: 140–52. [CrossRef]

Baudry, Maximilien, and Christian Y. Robert. 2017. Non Parametric Individual Claim Reserving in Insurance. Working paper.

Breiman, Leo, Friedman Jerome, Olshen Richard, and Stone Charles. 1984. *Classification and Regression Trees*. Wadsworth Statistics/Probability Series; New York: Routledge.

Buhlmann, Hans, Rene Schnieper, and Erwin Straub. 1980. Claims reserves in casualty insurance based on a probabilistic model. *Bulletin of the Association of Swiss Actuaries* 80: 21–45.

Charpentier, Arthur, and Mathieu Pigeon. 2016. Macro vs. micro methods in non-life claims reserving (an econometric perspective). *Risks* 4: 12. [CrossRef]

Chen, Tianqi, and Carlos Guestrin. 2016. Xgboost: A scalable tree boosting system. Paper presented at 22nd ACM SIGKDD International Conference on Knowledge Discovery and Data Mining, San Francisco, CA, USA, August 13–17; pp. 785–94.

De Jong, Piet, and Gillian Z. Heller. 2008. *Generalized Linear Models for Insurance Data*. Cambridge: Cambridge University Press.

England, Peter D., and Richard J. Verrall. 2002. Stochastic claims reserving in general insurance. *British Actuarial Journal* 8: 443–544. [CrossRef]

Friedman, Jerome H. 2001. Greedy function approximation: A gradient boosting machine. *Annals of Statistics* 29: 1189–232. [CrossRef]

Gabrielli, Andrea, Ronald Richman, and Mario V. Wüthrich. 2019. Neural Network Embedding of the Over-Dispersed Poisson Reserving Model. *Scandinavian Actuarial Journal* 2019: 1–29. [CrossRef]

Haastrup, Svend, and Elja Arjas. 1996. Claims reserving in continuous time; a nonparametric bayesian approach. *ASTIN Bulletin* 26: 139–64. [CrossRef]

Hachemeister, Charles. 1980. A stochastic model for loss reserving. *Transactions of the 21st International Congress of Actuaries* 1: 185–94.

Hesselager, Ole. 1994. A Markov model for loss reserving. *ASTIN Bulletin* 24: 183–93. [CrossRef]

Hiabu, Munir, Margraf Carolin, Martínez-Miranda Maria, and Nielsen Jens Perch. 2016. The link between classical reserving and granular reserving through double chain ladder and its extensions. *British Actuarial Journal* 21: 97–116. [CrossRef]

Huang, Jinlong, Chunjuan Qiu, and Xianyi Wu. 2015. Stochastic loss reserving in discrete time: Individual vs. aggregate data models. *Communications in Statistics—Theory and Methods* 44: 2180–206. [CrossRef]

Jewell, William S. 1989. Predicting IBNYR events and delays. *ASTIN Bulletin* 19: 25–55. [CrossRef]

Larsen, Christian Roholte. 2007. An individual claims reserving model. *ASTIN Bulletin* 37: 113–32. [CrossRef]

Lopez, Olivier, Xavier Milhaud, and Pierre-E. Thérond. 2016. Tree-based censored regression with applications in insurance. *Electronic Journal of Statistics* 10: 2685–716. [CrossRef]

Mack, Thomas. 1993. Distribution-free calculation of the standard error of chain ladder reserve estimates. *ASTIN Bulletin: The Journal of the IAA* 23: 213–25. [CrossRef]

Norberg, Ragnar. 1986. A contribution to modeling of IBNR claims. *Scandinavian Actuarial Journal* 1986: 155–203. [CrossRef]

Norberg, Ragnar. 1993. Prediction of outstanding liabilities in non-life insurance. *ASTIN Bulletin* 23: 95–115. [CrossRef]

Norberg, Ragnar. 1999. Prediction of outstanding liabilities. II Model variations and extensions. *ASTIN Bulletin* 29: 5–25. [CrossRef]

Pigeon, Mathieu, Katrien Antonio, and Michel Denuit. 2013. Individual loss reserving with the multivariate skew normal framework. *ASTIN Bulletin* 43: 399–428. [CrossRef]

Taylor, Greg, Gráinne McGuire, and James Sullivan. 2008. Individual claim loss reserving conditioned by case estimates. *Annals of Actuarial Science* 3: 215–56. [CrossRef]

Wüthrich, Mario V. 2018. Machine learning in individual claims reserving. *Scandinavian Actuarial Journal*. in press.

Wüthrich, Mario V., and Michael Merz. 2008. *Stochastic Claims Reserving Methods in Insurance*. Zürich and Tübigen: Wiley.

Zhao, Xiaobing, and Xian Zhou. 2010. Applying copula models to individual claim loss reserving methods. *Insurance: Mathematics and Economics* 46: 290–99. [CrossRef]

Zhao, Xiaobing, Xian Zhou, and Jing Long Wang. 2009. Semiparametric model for prediction of individual claim loss reserving. *Insurance: Mathematics and Economics* 45: 1–8. [CrossRef]

© 2019 by the authors. Licensee MDPI, Basel, Switzerland. This article is an open access article distributed under the terms and conditions of the Creative Commons Attribution (CC BY) license (http://creativecommons.org/licenses/by/4.0/).

Article

DeepTriangle: A Deep Learning Approach to Loss Reserving

Kevin Kuo

Kasa AI, 3040 78th Ave SE #1271, Mercer Island, WA 98040, USA; kevin@kasa.ai

Received: 15 August 2019; Accepted: 12 September 2019; Published: 16 September 2019

Abstract: We propose a novel approach for loss reserving based on deep neural networks. The approach allows for joint modeling of paid losses and claims outstanding, and incorporation of heterogeneous inputs. We validate the models on loss reserving data across lines of business, and show that they improve on the predictive accuracy of existing stochastic methods. The models require minimal feature engineering and expert input, and can be automated to produce forecasts more frequently than manual workflows.

Keywords: loss reserving; machine learning; neural networks

1. Introduction

In the loss reserving exercise for property and casualty insurers, actuaries are concerned with forecasting future payments due to claims. Accurately estimating these payments is important from the perspectives of various stakeholders in the insurance industry. For the management of the insurer, the estimates of unpaid claims inform decisions in underwriting, pricing, and strategy. For the investors, loss reserves, and transactions related to them, are essential components in the balance sheet and income statement of the insurer. In addition, for the regulators, accurate loss reserves are needed to appropriately understand the financial soundness of the insurer.

There can be time lags both for reporting of claims, where the insurer is not notified of a loss until long after it has occurred, and for final development of claims, where payments continue long after the loss has been reported. Also, the amounts of claims are uncertain before they have fully developed. These factors contribute to the difficulty of the loss reserving problem, for which extensive literature exists and active research is being done. We refer the reader to England and Verrall (2002) for a survey of the problem and existing techniques.

Deep learning has garnered increasing interest in recent years due to successful applications in many fields (LeCun et al. 2015) and has recently made its way into the loss reserving literature. Wüthrich (2018b) augments the traditional chain ladder method with neural networks to incorporate claims features, Gabrielli and Wüthrich (2018) use neural networks to syntheisze claims data, and Gabrielli et al. (2018) and Gabrielli (2019) embed classical parametric loss reserving models into neural networks. More specifically, the development in Gabrielli et al. (2018) and Gabrielli (2019) proposes initializing a neural network so that, before training, it corresponds exactly to a classical model, such as the over-dispersed Poisson model. The training iterations then adjust the weights of the neural network to minimize the prediction errors, which can be interpreted as a boosting procedure.

In developing our framework, which we call DeepTriangle[1], we also draw inspiration from the existing stochastic reserving literature. Works that propose using data in addition to paid losses include Quarg and Mack (2004), which uses incurred losses, and Miranda et al. (2012), which incorporates

---

[1] A portmanteau of *deep learning* and *loss development triangle*.

claim count information. Moving beyond a single homogeneous portfolio, (Avanzi et al. (2016)) considers the dependencies among lines of business within an insurer's portfolio, while Peremans et al. (2018) proposes a robust general multivariate chain ladder approach to accommodate outliers. There is also a category of models, referred to as state space or adaptive models, that allow parameters to evolve recursively in time as more data is observed (Chukhrova and Johannssen 2017). This iterative updating mechanism is similar in spirit to the continuous updating of neural network weights during model deployment.

The approach that we develop differs from existing works in many ways, and has the following advantages. First, it enables joint modeling of paid losses and claims outstanding for multiple companies simultaneously in a single model. In fact, the architecture can also accommodate arbitrary additional inputs, such as claim count data and economic indicators, should they be available to the modeler. Second, it requires no manual input during model updates or forecasting, which means that predictions can be generated more frequently than traditional processes, and, in turn, allows management to react to changes in the portfolio sooner.

The rest of the paper is organized as follows: Section 2 provides a brief overview of neural network terminology, Section 3 discusses the dataset used and introduces the proposed neural network architecture, Section 4 defines the performance metrics we use to benchmark our models and discuss the results, and Section 5 concludes.

2. Neural Network Preliminaries

For comprehensive treatments of neural network mechanics and implementation, we refer the reader to Goodfellow et al. (2016) and Chollet and Allaire (2018). A more actuarially oriented discussion can be found in Wuthrich and Buser (2019). To establish common terminology used in this paper, we present a brief overview in this section.

We motivate the discussion by considering an example feedforward network with fully connected layers represented in Figure 1, where the goal is to predict an output y from input x. The intermediate values, known as hidden layers and represented by $h_j^{[l]}$, try to transform the input data into representations that successively become more useful at predicting the output. The nodes in the figure are computed, for each layer $l = 1, \ldots, L$, as

$$h_j^{[l]} = g^{[l]}(z_j^{[l]}), \qquad (1)$$

where

$$z_j^{[l]} = w_j^{[l]T} h^{[l-1]} + b_j^{[l]}, \qquad (2)$$

for $j = 1, \ldots, n^{[l]}$. In these equations, a superscript $[l]$ denotes association with the layer l, a subscript j denotes association with the j-th component of the layer, of which there are $n^{[l]}$. The $g^{[l]}$ ($l = 1, \ldots, L$) are called activation functions, whose values $h^{[l]}$ are known as activations. The vectors $w_j^{[l]}$ and scalars $b_j^{[l]}$ are known as weights and biases, respectively, and together represent the parameters of the neural network, which are learned during training.

For $l = 1$, we define the previous layer activations as the input, so that the calculation for the first hidden layer becomes

$$h_j^{[1]} = g^{[1]}(w_j^{[1]T} x + b_j^{[1]}). \qquad (3)$$

Also, for the output layer $l = L$, we compute the prediction

$$\hat{y} = h_j^{[L]} = g^{[L]}(w_j^{[L]T} h^{[L-1]} + b_j^{[L]}). \qquad (4)$$

We can then think of a neural network as a sequence of function compositions $f = f_L \circ f_{L-1} \circ \cdots \circ f_1$ parameterized as $f(x; W^{[1]}, b^{[1]}, \ldots, W^{[L]}, b^{[L]})$. Here, it should be mentioned that the $g^{[l]}$ ($l = 1, \ldots, L$) are chosen to be nonlinear, except for possibly in the output layer. These nonlinearities are key to the success of neural networks, because otherwise we would have a trivial composition of linear models.

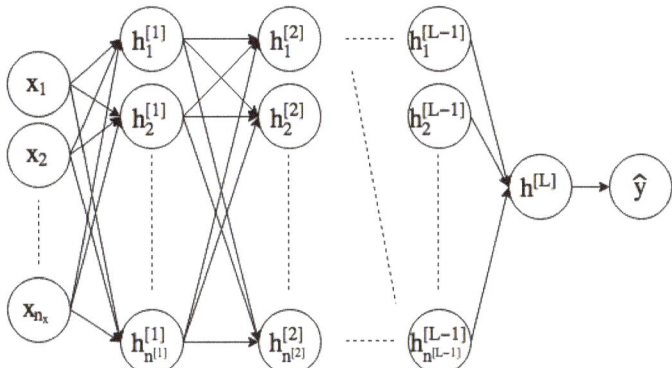

Figure 1. Feedforward neural network.

Each neural network model is specified with a specific loss function, which is used to measure how close the model predictions are to the actual values. During model training, the parameters discussed above are iteratively updated in order to minimize the loss function. Each update of the parameters typically involves only a subset, or mini-batch, of the training data, and one complete pass through the training data, which includes many updates, is known as an epoch. Training a neural network often requires many passes through the data.

3. Data and Model Architecture

In this section, we discuss the dataset used for our experiments and the proposed model architecture.

3.1. Data Source

We use the National Association of Insurance Commissioners (NAIC) Schedule P triangles (Meyers and Shi 2011). The dataset corresponds to claims from accident years 1988–1997, with development experience of 10 years for each accident year. In Schedule P data, the data is aggregated into accident year-development year records. The procedure for constructing the dataset is detailed in Meyers (2015).

Following Meyers (2015), we restrict ourselves to a subset of the data which covers four lines of business (commercial auto, private personal auto, workers' compensation, and other liability) and 50 companies in each line of business. This is done to facilitate comparison to existing results.

We use the following variables from the dataset in our study: line of business, company code, accident year, development lag, incurred loss, cumulative paid loss, and net earned premium. Claims outstanding, for the purpose of this study, is derived as incurred loss less cumulative paid loss. The company code is a categorical variable that denotes which insurer the records are associated with.

3.2. Training/Testing Setup

Let indices $1 \leq i \leq I$ denote accident years and $1 \leq j \leq J$ denote development years under consideration. Also, let $\{P_{i,j}\}$ and $\{OS_{i,j}\}$ denote the *incremental* paid losses and the *total* claims outstanding, or case reserves, respectively.

Then, at the end of calendar year I, we have access to the observed data

$$\{P_{i,j} : i = 1, \ldots, I; j = 1, \ldots, I - i + 1\} \tag{5}$$

and
$$\{OS_{i,j} : i = 1, \ldots, I; j = 1, \ldots, I - i + 1\}. \tag{6}$$

Assume that we are interested in development through the Ith development year; in other words, we only forecast through the eldest maturity in the available data. The goal then is to obtain predictions for future values $\{\widehat{P}_{i,j} : i = 2, \ldots, I; j = i + 1, \ldots, I\}$ and $\{\widehat{OS}_{i,j} : i = 2, \ldots, I; j = i + 1, \ldots, I\}$. We can then determine ultimate losses (UL) for each accident year $i = 1, \ldots, I$ by calculating

$$\widehat{UL}_i = \left(\sum_{j=1}^{I-i+1} P_{i,j} \right) + \left(\sum_{j=I-i+2}^{I} \widehat{P}_{i,j} \right). \tag{7}$$

In our case, data as of year end 1997 is used for training. We then evaluate predictive performance on the development year 10 cumulative paid losses.

3.3. Response and Predictor Variables

In DeepTriangle, each training sample is associated with an accident year-development year pair, which we refer to thereinafter as a *cell*. The response for the sample associated with accident year i and development year j is the sequence

$$(Y_{i,j}, Y_{i,j+1}, \ldots, Y_{i,I-i+1}), \tag{8}$$

where each $Y_{i,j} = (P_{i,j}/NPE_i, OS_{i,j}/NPE_i)$, and NPE_i denotes the net earned premium for accident year i. Working with loss ratios makes training more tractable by normalizing values into a similar scale.

The predictor for the sample contains two components. The first component is the observed history as of the end of the calendar year associated with the cell:

$$(Y_{i,1}, Y_{i,2}, \ldots, Y_{i,j-1}). \tag{9}$$

In other words, for each accident year and at each evaluation date for which we have data, we attempt to predict future development of the accident year's paid losses and claims outstanding based on the observed history as of that date. While we are ultimately interested in $P_{i,j}$, the paid losses, we include claims outstanding as an auxiliary output of the model. We elaborate on the reasoning behind this approach in the next section.

The second component of the predictor is the company identifier associated with the experience. Because we include experience from multiple companies in each training iteration, we need a way to differentiate the data from different companies. We discuss handling of the company identifier in more detail in the next section.

3.4. Model Architecture

As shown in Figure 2, DeepTriangle is a multi-task network (Caruana 1997) using a sequence-to-sequence architecture (Srivastava et al. 2015; Sutskever et al. 2014) with two prediction goals: paid loss and claims outstanding. We construct one model for each line of business and each model is trained on data from multiple companies.

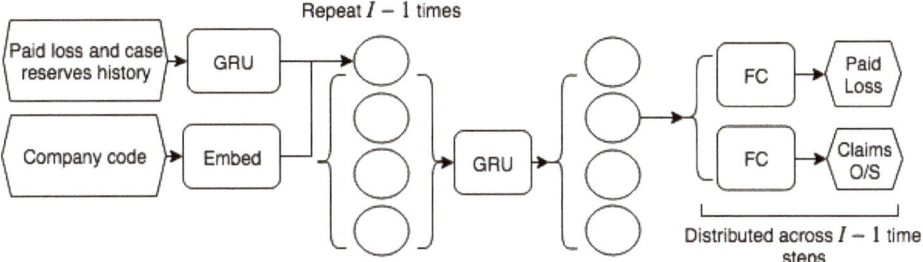

Figure 2. DeepTriangle architecture. *Embed* denotes embedding layer, *GRU* denotes gated recurrent unit, *FC* denotes fully connected layer.

3.4.1. Multi-Task Learning

Since the two target quantities, paid loss and claims outstanding, are related, we expect to obtain better performance by jointly training than predicting each quantity independently. While Caruana (1997) contains detailed discourse on the specific mechanisms of multi-task learning, we provide some heuristics on why it may improve predictions: by using the response data for claims outstanding, we are effectively increasing the training data size since we are providing more signals to the learning algorithm; there may be hidden features, useful for predicting paid losses, that are more easily learned by trying to predict claims outstanding; also, by trying to predict claims outstanding during training, we are imposing a bias towards neural network weight configurations which perform that task well, which lessens the likelihood of arriving at a model that overfits to random noise.

3.4.2. Sequential Input Processing

For handling the time series of paid losses and claims outstanding, we use gated recurrent units (GRU) (Chung et al. 2014), which is a type of recurrent neural network (RNN) building block that is appropriate for sequential data. A graphical representation of a GRU is shown in Figure 3, and the associated equations are as follows[2]:

$$\tilde{h}^{<t>} = \tanh(W_h[\Gamma_r h^{<t-1>}, x^{<t>}] + b_h) \tag{10}$$

$$\Gamma_r^{<t>} = \sigma(W_r[h^{<t-1>}, x^{<t>}] + b_r) \tag{11}$$

$$\Gamma_u^{<t>} = \sigma(W_u[h^{<t-1>}, x^{<t>}] + b_u) \tag{12}$$

$$h^{<t>} = \Gamma_u^{<t>} \tilde{h}^{<t>} + (1 - \Gamma_u^{<t>}) h^{<t-1>}. \tag{13}$$

Here, $h^{<t>}$ and $x^{<t>}$ represent the activation and input values, respectively, at time t, and σ denotes the logistic sigmoid function defined as

$$\sigma(x) = \frac{1}{1 + \exp(-x)}. \tag{14}$$

W_h, W_r, W_u, b_h, b_r, and b_u are the appropriately sized weight matrices and biases to be learned. Intuitively, the activations $h^{<t>}$ provide a way for the network to maintain state and "remember" values from early values of the input sequence. The values $\tilde{h}^{<t>}$ can be thought of as candidates to replace the current state, and $\Gamma_u^{<t>}$ determines the weighting between the previous state and the candidate state. We remark that although the GRU (and RNN in general) may seem opaque at first,

---

[2] Note the use of angle brackets to index position in a sequence rather than layers in a feedforward neural network as in Section 2.

they contain sequential instructions for updating weights just like vanilla feedforward neural networks (and can in fact be interpreted as such (Goodfellow et al. 2016)).

We first encode the sequential predictor with a GRU to obtain a summary encoding of the historical values. We then repeat the output $I - 1$ times before passing them to a decoder GRU that outputs its hidden state for each time step. The factor $I - 1$ is chosen here because for the Ith accident year, we need to forecast $I - 1$ timesteps into the future. For both the encoder and decoder GRU modules, we use 128 hidden units and a dropout rate of 0.2. Here, dropout refers to the regime where, during training, at each iteration, we randomly set the output of the hidden units to zero with a specified probability, in order to reduce overfitting (Srivastava et al. 2014). Intuitively, dropout accomplishes this by approximating an ensemble of sub-networks that can be constructed by removing some hidden units.

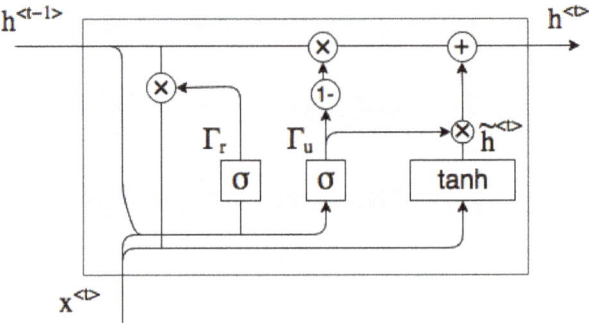

Figure 3. Gated recurrent unit.

3.4.3. Company Code Embeddings

The company code input is first passed to an embedding layer. In this process, each company is mapped to a fixed length vector in $\mathbb{R}^k$, where k is a hyperparameter. In our case, we choose $k =$ number of levels $- 1 = 49$, as recommended in Guo and Berkhahn (2016). In other words, each company is represented by a vector in $\mathbb{R}^{49}$. This mapping mechanism is part of the neural network and hence is learned during the training of the network, instead of in a separate data preprocessing step, so the learned numerical representations are optimized for predicted the future paid losses. Companies that are similar in the context of our claims forecasting problem are mapped to vectors that are close to each other in terms of Euclidean distance. Intuitively, one can think of this representation as a proxy for characteristics of the companies, such as size of book and case reserving philosophy. Categorical embedding is a common technique in deep learning that has been successfully applied to recommendation systems (Cheng et al. 2016) and retail sales prediction (Guo and Berkhahn 2016). In the actuarial science literature, Richman and Wuthrich (2018) use embedding layers to capture characteristics of regions in mortality forecasting, while Gabrielli et al. (2018) apply them to lines of business factors in loss reserving.

3.4.4. Fully Connected Layers and Outputs

Each timestep of the decoded sequence from the GRU decoder is then concatenated with the company embedding output. The concatenated values are then passed to two subnetworks of fully connected layers, each of which shares weights across the timesteps. The two subnetworks correspond to the paid loss and case outstanding predictions, respectively, and each consists of a hidden layer of 64 units with a dropout rate of 0.2, followed by an output layer of 1 unit to represent the paid loss or claims outstanding at a time step.

Rectified linear unit (ReLU) (Nair and Hinton 2010), defined as

$$x \mapsto \max(0, x), \tag{15}$$

is used as the activation function (which we denote by g in Section 2) for all fully connected layers, including both of the output layers. We remark that this choice of output activation implies we only predict nonnegative cash flows, i.e., no recoveries. This assumption is reasonable for the dataset we use in our experiments, but may be modified to accommodate other use cases.

3.5. Deployment Considerations

While one may not have access to the latest experience data of competitors, the company code predictor can be used to incorporate data from companies within a group insurer. During training, the relationships among the companies are inferred based on historical development behavior. This approach provides an automated and objective alternative to manually aggregating, or clustering, the data based on knowledge of the degree of homogeneity among the companies.

If new companies join the portfolio, or if the companies and associated claims are reorganized, one would modify the embedding input size to accommodate the new codes, leaving the rest of the architecture unchanged, then refit the model. The network would then assign embedding vectors to the new companies.

Since the model outputs predictions for each triangle cell, one can calculate the traditional age-to-age, or loss development, factors (LDF) using the model forecasts. Having a familiar output may enable easier integration of DeepTriangle into existing actuarial workflows.

Insurers often have access to richer information than is available in regulatory filings, which underlies the experiments in this paper. For example, in addition to paid and incurred losses, one may include claim count triangles so that the model can also learn from, and predict, frequency information.

4. Experiments

We now describe the performance metrics for benchmarking the models and training details, then discuss the results.

4.1. Evaluation Metrics

We aim to produce scalar metrics to evaluate the performance of the model on each line of business. To this end, for each company and each line of business, we calculate the actual and predicted ultimate losses as of development year 10, for all accident years combined, then compute the root mean squared percentage error (RMSPE) and mean absolute percentage error (MAPE) over companies in each line of business. Percentage errors are used in order to have unit-free measures for comparing across companies with vastly different sizes of portfolios. Formally, if C_l is the set of companies in line of business l,

$$MAPE_l = \frac{1}{|C_l|} \sum_{C \in C_l} \left| \frac{\widehat{UL}_C - UL_C}{UL_C} \right|, \tag{16}$$

and

$$RMSPE_l = \sqrt{\frac{1}{|C_l|} \sum_{C \in C_l} \left(\frac{\widehat{UL}_C - UL_C}{UL_C} \right)^2} \tag{17}$$

where $\widehat{UL}_C$ and UL_C are the predicted and actual cumulative ultimate losses, respectively, for company C.

An alternative approach for evaluation could involve weighting the company results by the associated earned premium or using dollar amounts. However, due to the distribution of company sizes in the dataset, the weights would concentrate on a handful of companies. Hence, to obtain a more balanced evaluation, we choose to report the unweighted percentage-based measures outlined above. We note that the evaluation of reserving models is an ongoing area of research; and refer the reader to Martinek (2019) for a recent analysis.

4.2. Implementation and Training

The loss function is computed as the average over the forecasted time steps of the mean squared error of the predictions. The losses for the outputs are then averaged to obtain the network loss. Formally, for the sample associated with cell (i, j), we can write the per-sample loss as

$$\frac{1}{I-i+1-(j-1)} \sum_{k=j}^{I-i+1} \frac{(\widehat{P_{i,k}} - P_{i,k})^2 + (\widehat{OS_{i,k}} - OS_{i,k})^2}{2}. \tag{18}$$

For optimization, we use the AMSGRAD (Reddi et al. 2018) variant of ADAM with a learning rate of 0.0005. We train each neural network for a maximum of 1000 epochs with the following early stopping scheme: if the loss on the validation set does not improve over a 200-epoch window, we terminate training and revert back to the weights on the epoch with the lowest validation loss. The validation set used in the early stopping criterion is defined to be the subset of the training data that becomes available after calendar year 1995. For each line of business, we create an ensemble of 100 models, each trained with the same architecture but different random weight initialization. This is done to reduce the variance inherent in the randomness associated with neural networks.

We implement DeepTriangle using the keras R package (Chollet et al. 2017) and TensorFlow (Abadi et al. 2015), which are open source software for developing neural network models. Code for producing the experiment results is available online.[3]

4.3. Results and Discussion

In Table 1 we tabulate the out-of-time performance of DeepTriangle against other models: the Mack chain-ladder model (Mack 1993), the bootstrap ODP model (England and Verrall 2002), an AutoML model, and a selection of Bayesian Markov chain Monte Carlo (MCMC) models from Meyers (2015) including the correlated incremental trend (CIT) and leveled incremental trend (LIT) models. For the stochastic models, we use the means of the predictive distributions as the point estimates to which we compare the actual outcomes. For DeepTriangle, we report the averaged predictions from the ensembles.

Table 1. Performance comparison of various models. DeepTriangle and AutoML are abbreviated to DT and ML, respectively. The best metric for each line of business is in bold.

Line of Business	Mack	ODP	CIT	LIT	ML	DT
MAPE						
Commercial Auto	0.060	0.217	0.052	0.052	0.068	**0.043**
Other Liability	0.134	0.223	0.165	0.152	0.142	**0.109**
Private Passenger Auto	0.038	0.039	0.038	0.040	0.036	**0.025**
Workers' Compensation	0.053	0.105	0.054	0.054	0.067	**0.046**
RMSPE						
Commercial Auto	0.080	0.822	0.076	0.074	0.096	**0.057**
Other Liability	0.202	0.477	0.220	0.209	0.181	**0.150**
Private Passenger Auto	0.061	0.063	0.057	0.060	0.059	**0.039**
Workers' Compensation	0.079	0.368	0.080	0.080	0.099	**0.067**

---

[3] https://github.com/kasaai/deeptriangle.

The AutoML model is developed by automatically searching over a set of common machine learning techniques. In the implementation we use, it trains and cross-validates a random forest, an extremely randomized forest, a random grid of gradient boosting machines, a random grid of deep feedforward neural networks, and stacked ensembles thereof (The H2O.ai team 2018). Details of these algorithms can be found in Friedman et al. (2001). Because the machine learning techniques produce scalar outputs, we use an iterative forecasting scheme where the prediction for a timestep is used in the predictor for the next timestep.

We see that DeepTriangle improves the performance of the popular chain ladder and ODP models, common machine learning models, and Bayesian stochastic models.

In addition to aggregated results for all companies, we also investigate qualitatively the ability of DeepTriangle to learn development patterns of individual companies. Figures 4 and 5 show the paid loss development and claims outstanding development for the commercial auto line of Company 1767 and the workers' compensation line of Company 337, respectively. We see that the model captures the development patterns for Company 1767 reasonably well. However, it is unsuccessful in forecasting the deteriorating loss ratios for Company 337's workers' compensation book.

We do not study uncertainty estimates in this paper nor interpret the forecasts as posterior predictive distributions; rather, they are included to reflect the stochastic nature of optimizing neural networks. We note that others have exploited randomness in weight initialization in producing predictive distributions (Lakshminarayanan et al. 2017), and further research could study the applicability of these techniques to reserve variability.

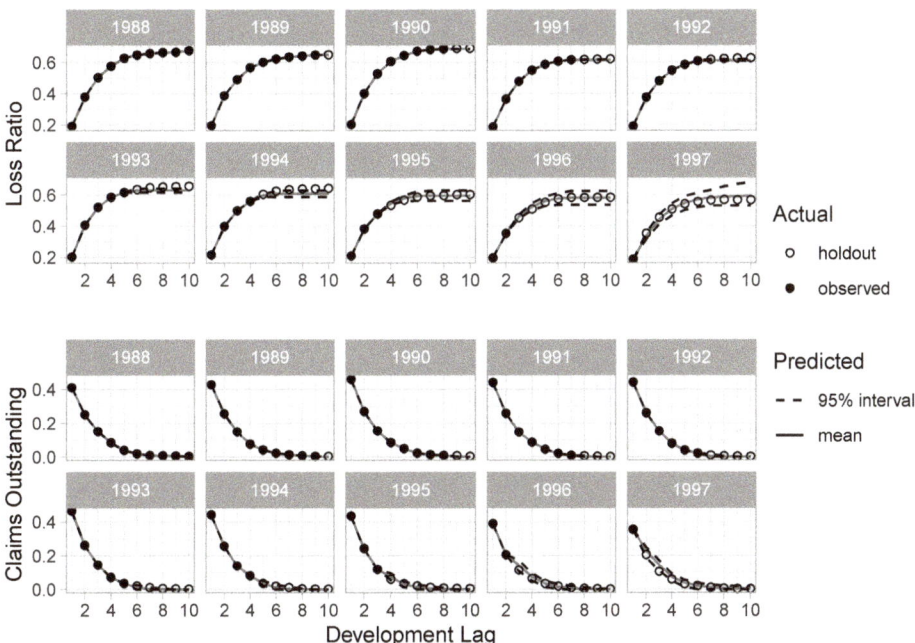

Figure 4. Development by accident year for Company 1767, commercial auto.

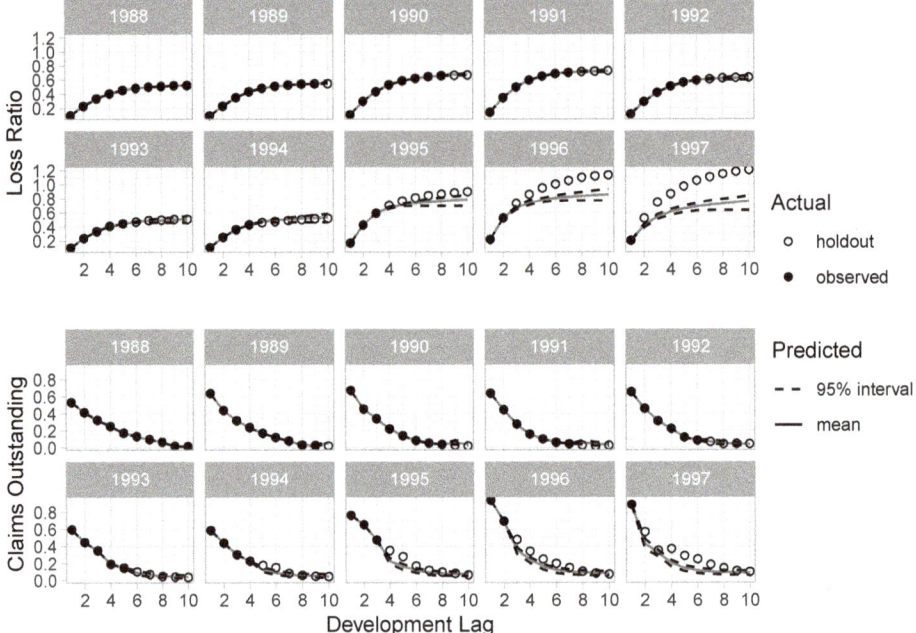

Figure 5. Development by accident year for Company 337, workers' compensation.

5. Conclusions

We introduce DeepTriangle, a deep learning framework for forecasting paid losses. Our models are able to attain performance comparable, by our metrics, to modern stochastic reserving techniques, without expert input. This means that one can automate model updating and report production at the desired frequency (although we note that, as with any automated machine learning system, a process involving expert review should be implemented). By using neural networks, we can incorporate multiple heterogeneous inputs and train on multiple objectives simultaneously, and also allow customization of models based on available data. To summarize, this framework maintains accuracy while providing automatability and extensibility.

We analyze an aggregated dataset with limited features in this paper because it is publicly available and well studied, but one can extend DeepTriangle to incorporate additional data, such as claim counts.

Deep neural networks can be designed to extend recent efforts, such as Wüthrich (2018a), on applying machine learning to claims level reserving. They can also be designed to incorporate additional features that are not handled well by traditional machine learning algorithms, such as claims adjusters' notes from free text fields and images.

While this study focuses on prediction of point estimates, future extensions may include outputting distributions in order to address reserve variability.

Funding: This research received no external funding.

Acknowledgments: We thank Sigrid Keydana, Ronald Richman, the anonymous reviewers, and the volunteers on the Casualty Actuarial Society Committee on Reserves (CASCOR) who helped to improve the paper through helpful comments and discussions.

Conflicts of Interest: The author declares no conflict of interest.

References

Abadi, Martín, Ashish Agarwal, Paul Barham, Eugene Brevdo, Zhifeng Chen, Craig Citro, Greg S. Corrado, Andy Davis, Jeffrey Dean, Matthieu Devin, and et al. 2015. TensorFlow: Large-Scale Machine Learning on Heterogeneous Systems. *arXiv* arXiv:1603.04467.

Avanzi, Benjamin, Greg Taylor, Phuong Anh Vu, and Bernard Wong. 2016. Stochastic loss reserving with dependence: A flexible multivariate tweedie approach. *Insurance: Mathematics and Economics* 71: 63–78. [CrossRef]

Caruana, Rich. 1997. Multitask learning. *Machine Learning* 28: 41–75. [CrossRef]

Cheng, Heng-Tze, Mustafa Ispir, Rohan Anil, Zakaria Haque, Lichan Hong, Vihan Jain, Xiaobing Liu, Hemal Shah, Levent Koc, Jeremiah Harmsen, and et al. 2016. Wide & deep learning for recommender systems. In Proceedings of the 1st Workshop on Deep Learning for Recommender Systems—DLRS 2016, Boston, MA, USA, September 15. [CrossRef]

Chollet, Francois, and Joseph J. Allaire. 2018. *Deep Learning with R*. Shelter Island: Manning Publications.

Chollet, François, and Joseph J. Allaire. 2017. R Interface to Keras. Available online: https://github.com/rstudio/keras (accessed on 7 September 2019).

Chukhrova, Nataliya, and Arne Johannssen. 2017. State space models and the kalman-filter in stochastic claims reserving: Forecasting, filtering and smoothing. *Risks* 5: 30. [CrossRef]

Chung, Junyoung, Caglar Gulcehre, KyungHyun Cho, and Yoshua Bengio. 2014. Empirical evaluation of gated recurrent neural networks on sequence modeling. *arXiv* arXiv:1412.3555.

England, Peter D., and Richard J. Verrall. 2002. Stochastic claims reserving in general insurance. *British Actuarial Journal* 8: 443–518. [CrossRef]

Friedman, Jerome, Trevor Hastie, and Robert Tibshirani. 2001. *The Elements of Statistical Learning*. New York: Springer.

Gabrielli, Andrea. 2019. A Neural Network Boosted Double Over-Dispersed Poisson Claims Reserving Model. Available online: https://ssrn.com/abstract=3365517 (accessed on 15 September 2019).

Gabrielli, Andrea, Ronald Richman, and Mario V. Wuthrich. 2018. Neural Network Embedding of the Over-Dispersed Poisson Reserving Model. Available online: https://ssrn.com/abstract=3288454 (accessed on 15 September 2019).

Gabrielli, Andrea, and Mario V. Wüthrich. 2018. An individual claims history simulation machine. *Risks* 6: 29. [CrossRef]

Goodfellow, Ian, Yoshua Bengio, and Aaron Courville. 2016. *Deep Learning*. Cambridge: MIT Press.

Guo, Cheng, and Felix Berkhahn. 2016. Entity embeddings of categorical variables. *arXiv* arXiv:1604.06737.

Lakshminarayanan, Balaji, Alexander Pritzel, and Charles Blundell. 2017. Simple and scalable predictive uncertainty estimation using deep ensembles. In Proceedings of the Advances in Neural Information Processing Systems 30, Long Beach, CA, USA, December 4–9.

LeCun, Yann, Yoshua Bengio, and Geoffrey Hinton. 2015. Deep learning. *Nature* 521: 436. [CrossRef] [PubMed]

Mack, Thomas. 1993. Distribution-free calculation of the standard error of chain ladder reserve estimates. *ASTIN Bulletin* 23: 213–25. [CrossRef]

Martinek, László. 2019. Analysis of stochastic reserving models by means of naic claims data. *Risks* 7: 62. [CrossRef]

Meyers, Glenn. 2015. *Stochastic Loss Reserving Using Bayesian MCMC Models*. Arlington: Casualty Actuarial Society.

Meyers, Glenn, and Peng Shi. 2011. Loss Reserving Data Pulled from NAIC Schedule p. Available online: http://www.casact.org/research/index.cfm?fa=loss_reserves_data (accessed on 7 September 2019).

Miranda, María Dolores Martínez, Jens Perch Nielsen, and Richard Verrall. 2012. Double chain ladder. *ASTIN Bulletin: The Journal of the IAA* 42: 59–76.

Nair, Vinod, and Geoffrey E. Hinton. 2010. Rectified linear units improve restricted boltzmann machines. In Proceedings of the 27th International Conference on Machine Learning, Haifa, Israel, June 21–24.

Peremans, Kris, Stefan Van Aelst, and Tim Verdonck. 2018. A robust general multivariate chain ladder method. *Risks* 6: 108. [CrossRef]

Quarg, Gerhard, and Thomas Mack. 2004. Munich chain ladder. *Blätter der DGVFM* 26: 597–630. [CrossRef]

Reddi, Sashank J., Satyen Kale, and Sanjiv Kumar. 2018. On the convergence of adam and beyond. In Proceedings of the 6th International Conference on Learning Representations, Vancouver, BC, Canada, April 30–May 3.

Richman, Ronald, and Mario V. Wuthrich. 2018. A Neural Network Extension of the Lee-Carter Model to Multiple Populations. Available online: https://ssrn.com/abstract=3270877 (accessed on 7 September 2019).

Srivastava, Nitish, Geoffrey Hinton, Alex Krizhevsky, Ilya Sutskever, and Ruslan Salakhutdinov. 2014. Dropout: A simple way to prevent neural networks from overfitting. *The Journal of Machine Learning Research* 15: 1929–58.

Srivastava, Nitish, Elman Mansimov, and Ruslan Salakhutdinov. 2015. Unsupervised learning of video representations using LSTMs. *arXiv* arXiv:1502.04681.

Sutskever, Ilya, Oriol Vinyals, and Quoc V. Le. 2014. Sequence to sequence learning with neural networks. In Proceedings of the Advances in Neural Information Processing Systems 27, Montreal, QC, Canada, December 8–13.

The H2O.ai team. 2018. *h2o: R Interface for H2O*. R Package Version 3.20.0.8. Mountain View: H2O.ai.

Wüthrich, Mario V. 2018a. Machine learning in individual claims reserving. *Scandinavian Actuarial Journal* 1–16. [CrossRef]

Wüthrich, Mario V. 2018b. Neural networks applied to chain–ladder reserving. *European Actuarial Journal* 8: 407–36. [CrossRef]

Wuthrich, Mario V., and Christoph Buser. 2019. Data analytics for non-life insurance pricing. *Swiss Finance Institute Research Paper*. doi:10.2139/ssrn.2870308. [CrossRef]

© 2019 by the author. Licensee MDPI, Basel, Switzerland. This article is an open access article distributed under the terms and conditions of the Creative Commons Attribution (CC BY) license (http://creativecommons.org/licenses/by/4.0/).

Article

Penalising Unexplainability in Neural Networks for Predicting Payments per Claim Incurred

Jacky H. L. Poon

Independent Researcher, Level 18, 1 Farrer Place, Sydney, NSW 2000, Australia; jackypn@gmail.com

Received: 13 June 2019; Accepted: 23 August 2019; Published: 1 September 2019

Abstract: In actuarial modelling of risk pricing and loss reserving in general insurance, also known as P&C or non-life insurance, there is business value in the predictive power and automation through machine learning. However, interpretability can be critical, especially in explaining to key stakeholders and regulators. We present a granular machine learning model framework to jointly predict loss development and segment risk pricing. Generalising the Payments per Claim Incurred (PPCI) loss reserving method with risk variables and residual neural networks, this combines interpretable linear and sophisticated neural network components so that the 'unexplainable' component can be identified and regularised with a separate penalty. The model is tested for a real-life insurance dataset, and generally outperformed PPCI on predicting ultimate loss for sufficient sample size.

Keywords: actuarial; risk pricing; loss reserving; granular models; neural networks; payments per claim incurred

---

1. Introduction

1.1. Rationale

Key business goals for claims models typically include predictive power, automation and ease of use, and interpretability. Predictive power is valuable in any model, but for risk pricing in insurance, higher accuracy leads to selecting lower cost risks and is consequently a competitive advantage. Machine learning and automation improves the business efficiency of the modelling process, and also facilitates models with large numbers of parameters that can reflect complex non-linear relationships. Finally, interpretability is important for communications to business stakeholders and to regulators, particularly in loss reserving to justify projections.

Common actuarial industry practice at the time of writing is for separate sophisticated risk pricing models and relatively simple reserving models. Risk pricing models are typically granular claims models—traditionally Generalised Linear Models ('GLM'). Increasingly Gradient Boosting Decision Trees/Machines ('GBM') have become a popular alternative. Machine learning approaches allow automated identification and fitting of non-linear effects. These can contribute to a higher accuracy than GLM approaches, at the cost of transparency. Conversely, reserving models typically use simple, deterministic triangulation based approaches, with selections based on actuarial judgement. The simplicity of a portfolio approach for loss reserving has the advantages of transparency and the ability to manually adjust selections based on actuarial judgement.

However, separate risk pricing and reserving models can present practical challenges, and results can be circular. In creating risk pricing models, a rescaling adjustment based on reserving is often required to the recent, undeveloped data. In creating reserving models, the pricing view is often used as an initial prior for methods such as Bornhuetter–Ferguson.

Business stakeholders also often demand detailed segmented views on loss ratios to assist in decision-making on underwriting and portfolio management processes, for which a portfolio approach may not be appropriate. Also, where there has been a significant mix shift in the risks insured—perhaps due to growth or shrinkage in particular segments—the portfolio approach breaks down and input from a granular view (often the pricing view) is needed. This suggests that a granular approach to reserving incorporating detailed policy or claims data should be able to model segmented results with better accuracy than simple allocation methods of portfolio Incurred But Not Reported (IBNR) reserves.

1.2. Granular Claims Models

Subsequently, a number of papers have emerged for granular model reserving. An earlier example is a GLM approach, using explanatory variables with conditioning for case estimates (Taylor et al. 2008).

Regularisation via *l*1 and *l*2 losses are heavily used as a machine learning technique, both at the portfolio level for loss reserving (Miller et al. 2016), or at the granular level to select factors, fit splines or apply other useful constraints to otherwise overparametrised models (Semenovich et al. 2010).

1.3. Neural Networks

Neural network based architectures are extremely flexible and enables use of data in formats such as numerical, categorical, image, time series, and freeform text data. It also allows multiple concurrent outputs using multi-task neural networks (e.g., Fotso 2018; Poon 2018), as well as outputs of a time series using recurrent neural network components such as the gated recurrent unit (Kuo 2018).

However, explainability is an issue when applying this model to claims, as fully connected neural layers can contain large numbers of parameters. Attempts have been made at structuring the network in a more explainable way in other applications, such as constraining neural components to have only a single input and output neuron (Vaughan et al. 2018), or recovering explainability of individual predictions through locally interpretable linear approximations (Ribeiro et al. 2016), but no approach has emerged as an industry standard to date, and it remains unclear whether a fully explainable model structure that preserves the predictive ability of a standard neural network is possible.

1.4. Residual Neural Networks

Residual networks ('ResNets') are a type of neural networks originally introduced in vision recognition (He et al. 2015). This allows training of deeper networks for state-of-the-art performance, but has found value in other applications, including actuarial modelling (Schelldorfer and Wuthrich 2019).

ResNets introduce the concept of 'skip connections', whereby an earlier layer is directly connected to a later layer (Figure 1). An observation is that for a network with a single residual block, the skip connection is in itself a linear model, ensembled with the neural network layers. With the exponential activation function, the linear model becomes a log-link GLM.

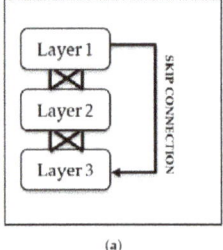
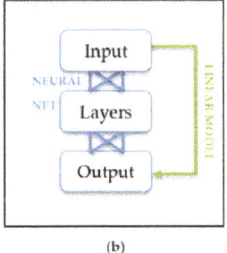

(a)   (b)

Figure 1. (a) A residual block comprising of a group of three layers, showing the skip connection, which can skip one or multiple layers; (b) The same block as a model, showing interpretable linear or GLM model and 'unexplainable' neural network.

Mathematically, the above residual block in Figure 1b can be expressed as follows:

Let B_1, B_2, B_3 and B_4 be weight matrices and $a(x)$ be the activation function. Examples of activation functions include the Rectified Linear Unit (ReLU):

$$a(x) = \max(0, x)$$

or the Scaled Exponential Linear Unit (SELU), which is used in the model later in this paper:

$$a(x) = \lambda \begin{cases} x & \text{if } x > 0 \\ ae^x - a & \text{if } x \leq 0 \end{cases}.$$

For a standard feed-forward neural network with two hidden layers, we find b_1, b_2, b_3 and b_4 to approximately minimise actual loss versus predicted $Loss(\hat{y}, y)$ where:

$$x_1 = a(B_1 \, x_{input}),$$

$$x_2 = a(B_2 \, x_1),$$

$$\hat{y}(B_1, B_2, B_3, x_{input}) = B_3 \, x_2.$$

However, for the residual network, the skip connection can be added to the output.

$$\hat{y}(B_1, B_2, B_3, B_4, x_{input}) = B_3 \, x_2 + B_4 \, x_{input}.$$

1.5. Embeddings

Embeddings are an encoding for categorical variables that is an alternative to one-hot encoding. Each label for a categorical factor is assigned a (typically) $1 \times n$ vector representation that can be trained with the model. For $n = 1$, each category corresponds with only one value, the embedding can produce results equivalent to one-hot encoding in an additive model structure.

1.6. Hyperparameter Selection

Layers of a neural network can be regularised separately, by applying a different λ hyperparameter for $l1$ or $l2$ regularisation loss to any of the B_1, B_2, B_3 and B_4 weights individually as above. For a given loss function $Loss(\hat{y}, y)$, a fully parametrised regularised loss function would be as below (the model in the next section uses mean-squared error loss):

$$RegLoss(\hat{y}, y) = Loss(\hat{y}, y) + \lambda_{1,1}|B_1| + \lambda_{1,2}|B_2| + \lambda_{1,3}|B_3| + \lambda_{1,4}|B_4| + \lambda_{2,1}|B_1|$$
$$+ \lambda_{2,2}|B_2| + \lambda_{2,3}|B_3| + \lambda_{2,4}|B_4|.$$

We discuss two approaches for selecting the regularisation parameters. The first is to optimise for holdout loss to find the most predictive model. One method to do so is a Random Grid Search, which tests random sets of hyperparameters and selects the model with the best holdout error, or Bayesian Optimisation, which estimates parameters via a Gaussian Process.

However, a second view is that regularisation provides a mechanism to penalise 'opaque' neural features in favour of 'transparent' linear features. When the regularisation parameters of the dense layers are set towards high values, the neural network components would shrink towards zero reducing the network to a linear model.

We put forward the concept that between the interpretable linear model and the residual network model, the regularisation parameter for residual network weights represents a continuum of models between those two competing objectives.

Also, by blending the residual model with the original model, we put forward the idea that the weights given to the linear model versus the residual network may potentially form a basis for evaluating the extent to which non-linear effects exist within the data—if the residual model is extremely effective, loss optimisation will bring the blend weight of the residual towards 1.0. Subsequently, the actuary should do additional manual analysis to improve interpretability. An iterative process of feature engineering such as creating splines for age could reduce the need for the opaque neural network component until the neural network is no longer needed.

However, in regards to penalising 'unexplainability' through regularising model components, an open question would be in regards to what economic value is to be assigned to interpretability of the model, such that an appropriate penalty can be applied.

With this in mind, we test this approach with a granular model that resembles a fully parametrised PPCI-like model, combining simple linear weights for interpretability with residual components for replicating non-linear effects.

2. Model

2.1. Definitions

Consider a dataset with dates, features, and claims development in the cross-tab format of Table 1:

Table 1. Training data format.

Origin Period	Feature 1	...	Feature m	Claim Reported by Delay			Claim Paid Reported by Delay			Data Exists Flag by Delay [1]		
		x		c			p			w		
				1	...	n	1	...	n	1	...	n
1 January 2015				1		0	0		$2000	1		1
1 December 2016		-		0		NaN	0		NaN	1		0
1 December 2015				0		1	0		$3000	1		1

[1] Exposure weights if needed would be multiplied to the data existence flag.

Features are policy and risk details—rating factors or any details relevant for the risk premium model. This includes origin period, the start dates of triangulation, typically be accident month, quarter or year. Numerical features are normalised to a mean of zero and variance of one, and categorical features are integers encoded for the embeddings.

Exposure weights allow a yearly policy to be divided into multiple monthly records with earned exposure.

Incremental claim count and payments data are matched back to the exposure record and is split into columns by delay period. Delay represents times from accident to the date of claim reporting (counts) or payment with a maximum tail of 'n' periods. Per standard actuarial practice, these are ideally adjusted for inflation.

Consequently, the dataset is structured such that

- The sum of 'claim counts reported by delay' by origin period is the incremental claims reported triangle,
- The sum of 'claim payments by delay' by origin period is the incremental payments triangle,
- If the claim counts and payments were the ultimates, it would be a typical GLM risk pricing dataset.
- The dataset remains reasonably compact as claims are in cross-tab format, which is beneficial from a memory usage perspective.

This allows us to jointly fit a risk pricing and loss reserving model. Let:

- x_i be features, for policy exposures i, including the accident or origin period,
- $w_{i,t}$ be exposure weights for exposure i in delay period t, with missing data after the balance date being weighted as 0,

- $C_{i,t}$ be claim count reported for the exposure in delay period t, with $C_i = \Sigma C_{i,t}$ and
- $P_{i,t}$ be claim payments for the exposure in delay period t, with $P_i = \Sigma P_{i,t}$.

We wish to build a model for $E(C_{i,t})$ and $E(P_{i,t})$ based on x and w.

2.2. From Payments Per Claim Incurrred to Granular Model

A traditional PPCI model predicts expected payments P at delay t as a ratio of ultimate incurred C:

$$E(P_{i,t}) = c_i\, q_t,$$

where c_i is an estimate of ultimate claim count, and q_t is the payments per claim incurred.

However, these payments per claim can be factored into the expected claim severity and the percentage paid in each period.

$$E(P_{i,t}) = c_i\, q\, b_t,\ \Sigma_t b_t = 1.$$

Consequently, the Payment per Claim Incurred model can be expressed as a simple frequency model (c), a constant claim severity model (q) and a constant percentage paid per period model (b).

In the model, we replace these with granular models for each, which also meets the needs of risk pricing to model frequency and severity by rating factors.

2.3. Network

The network diagram is shown in Figure 2.

In the interpretable model, linear models of total frequency and payments per policy were set as a function of the features. With B representing linear weights, let:

$$c_{linear} = B_c\, \mathbf{x}$$

With the exponential transform, they become GLMs. The payments per policy can also be set to follow the count logic for a risk premium model with $p_{linear} = B_p\, \mathbf{x}$ or a frequency-severity model by adding the frequency component at each step, such as with $p_{linear} = c_{linear} + B_p\, \mathbf{x}$.

To allocate that to the prediction of counts and payments at delay t, development parameters d_c and d_p were fitted with a log-softmax transform, let:

$$c_{interpretable,t} = w_{c,t} \times \exp(c + \log(\text{softmax}(d_{c,t}))).$$

The softmax transform enforces that the restriction that the sum of percentage developed is 100%. Without this constraint, it is possible for the expected claim count/paid to 'explode' with the percentage developed remaining at low values. In calculations, it is applied as logsoftmax due to numerical stability reasons.

Currently, the development function is fully parametrised but a future potential extension might be to apply a penalty for the percentage-developed distribution or splines to enforce smoothness of the development percentages.

Further parametrising the development network, such as using the xNNs (Vaughan et al.) explainable network splines could reduce the unexplainable components beyond the linear model used.

The 'neural model' is similar, except with the residual network components. The proposed network to predict expected frequency and cost per policy is set up with dense layers with outputs concatenated with the original inputs for the final linear model. Three dense layers is often considered to be sufficient for structured data problems but more can be added. For the model results below, SELU activation was used for stability reasons. Consequently, with b representing weight vectors, let:

$$n_1 = \text{SELU}(B_1\, \mathbf{x})$$

$$n_2 = \text{SELU}(B_2\, n_1)$$

$$n_3 = \text{SELU}(B_3\, n_2)$$

$$c_{\text{residual}} = B_4\, n_3$$

$$d_{\text{c-residual}} = B_5\, n_3$$

$$c_{\text{neural}, t} = w_{c,t} \times \exp(c_{\text{linear}} + c_{\text{residual}} + \log\_\text{softmax}(d_{c,t}))$$

Finally, a blended model is calculated by fitting a weighted average between the two models, with the weight constrained to be (0, 1) by fitting a parameter w_c such that:

$$\text{Weight}_c = \exp(w_c)/(1 + \exp(w_c)),$$

$$c_{\text{blended},t} = \text{Weight}_c\, c_{\text{interpretable},t} + (1 - \text{Weight}_c\, c_{\text{neural},t})$$

This is intended to provide an indication as to the explanatory power of the residual network compared to the simpler linear model. With optimised hyperparameters, one would expect residual network weights to converge to 1.0 if it always explained better than the linear model.

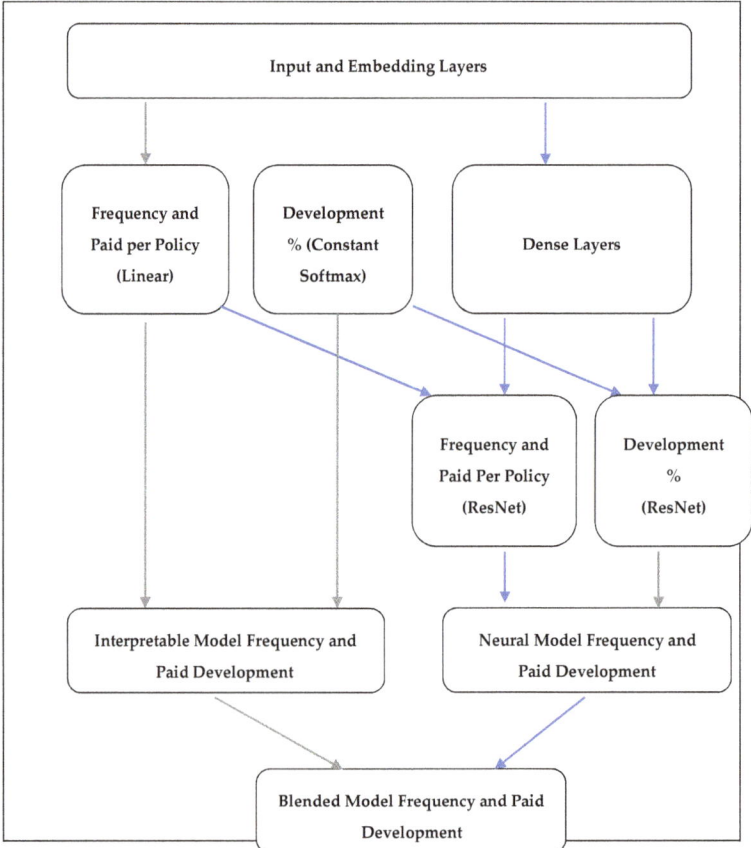

Figure 2. Simplified model network graph. Each block represents a group of layers, and the arrows represent the data flow. Grey arrows represent the "interpretable" network flow, whilst blue lines represent the "neural" network flow.

2.4. Loss

The loss function was set to optimise the sum of mean-squared error loss of all claims count and claims paid per policy for each of the interpretable, residual and blended networks in total, and the additional *l1* penalties for the linear risk pricing weights.

One issue with multi-task learning is that if losses are imbalanced, the optimisation may favour one particular set of outputs. While Poisson and Tweedie losses may be more appropriate for counts and payments, respectively, as a simplification, the Mean Squared Error (MSE) (with the exponential activation function) was used for all outputs to avoid having to significantly address this issue. The backpropogated gradients are similar. This may have been insufficient as some results seen later on may have optimised the claims paid, which have higher variation than claims count. More sophisticated approaches would be possible.

2.5. Training: Dropout, Optimiser, Shuffling, Batch Size, and Learn Rate Scheduler

A dropout layer (Srivastava et al. 2014) was applied for training the residual network, and Adam (Kingma and Ba 2015), an adaptive moment estimation optimiser, with separate *l2* weight decay penalties for the linear risk pricing and residual network weights, was used as the optimiser for the model. Training data was shuffled to reduce mix bias within each batch. A high batch size was used given the sparsity of the data to ensure sufficient claims data in each batch and gradient norm clipping was applied to improve stability of the training process. Weights initialisation to suitable starting values, learn rate search and the '1cycle' learn rate scheduler (Smith 2018) was used to speed up convergence.

2.6. Language and Package

The model was coded in Python using the Pytorch package. Pytorch was chosen for its high level API compared to Tensorflow, ease of customisation compared to Keras, stability, wide usage and availability of documentation. The version of the code used in this paper was uploaded to: https://github.com/JackyP/penalised-unexplainability-network-payments-per-claim-incurred/blob/1e757249e4f20a75e5e645d5a9f2a7ffb089a8a7/punppci/pytorch.py, with the intention to further develop and, should it reach a state of maturity, to publish in the Python repository PyPI as package 'punppci'.

3. Dataset Used

3.1. Dataset Details

The model was tested on actual proprietary policy and claim data with 6 features, approximately 250,000 policy exposure records underwritten in 2015–2016 calendar year and 32,000 claims, with claim reported counts and claim paid amounts developed over 24 development months.

For testing accuracy, claims reported or payments transacted after 31 December 2016 was censored for model fitting and used as holdout data.

3.2. Cleaning and Sampling

As part of data preparation, large claims were capped and then both claim frequency and payment was scaled by average frequency and paid per policy of the censored data—an initial estimate of portfolio averages that was free of data leakage from the holdout data. Features were normalised using mean-variance standardisation, with categorical features one-hot encoded for simplicity (although embeddings is recognised to be ideal).

The model was tested on samples of the data of 5000, 10,000, 25,000, 50,000, 100,000 and 200,000 policies with hyperparameters as detailed in Section 4 to test the models' effectiveness with various dataset sizes, and then on the full dataset with hyperparameter search.

3.3. Comparison with Manual Selections for Chain Ladder and PPCI

The benchmarking is against a mechanical (or naïve) application of chain ladder and PPCI. In practice, factor selections would be based on both actuarial judgement, with manual identification of unusual events, selection of averages where checks for accident or calendar year trends, and manual smoothing of factors.

Consequently, a manual review of the full dataset was also conducted to validate whether there were features that would influence manual selections; however, the triangles were fairly unremarkable given the short duration of the dataset over two accident years, reasonably large size of sample and short tail, non-statutory insurance portfolio. Certain product segments were known to develop slower; however, there was no significant mix shift towards or away from those segments during the period. Individual claim factors also did not appear to have any trends.

4. Results

4.1. Sampling Sizes

For the sampling test, linear $l1$ and $l2$ were set to 0.01, the residual network $l2$ was set to zero for weights and biases. For the full dataset, hyperparameters were firstly grouped into '$l1$ and $l2$ linear', '$l2$ residual' and '$l2$ bias', which were applied to both counts and paid for simplicity, and then Bayesian optimisation with the 'scikit-optimize' package was applied.

Table 2 shows the comparison of the squared error between actual versus expected ultimates for the model compared with naïve chain ladder and PPCI.

Table 2. Neural network versus traditional chain ladder and PPCI performance (lower is better).

Test	Sample Size	Seed	Chain Ladder SE Count	PPCI SE Paid	Model SE Count	Model SE Paid	Better Paid SE
0	5000	1	1453.14	3436.19	NaN	NaN	N
1	5000	2	472.17	2447.26	256.78	2183.37	Y
2	5000	3	431.78	5638.29	NaN	NaN	N
3	5000	4	339.55	1652.14	224.21	3401.45	N
4	5000	5	1590.66	58,388.27	NaN	NaN	N
5	10,000	1	540.19	4070.24	823.89	5181.73	N
6	10,000	2	2533.18	51,956.42	389.81	44,884.23	Y
7	10,000	3	606.79	11,418.01	272.21	7511.17	Y
8	10,000	4	1810.21	209,956.66	976.48	202,351.99	Y
9	10,000	5	1057.81	52,508.37	270.61	42,912.06	Y
10	25,000	1	5575.31	35,060.89	2583.43	23,732.57	Y
11	25,000	2	4644.56	61,120.81	750.18	51,177.28	Y
12	25,000	3	1969.43	295,767.11	NaN	NaN	N
13	25,000	4	4054.21	309,086.25	1985.41	299,889.39	Y
14	25,000	5	1703.19	57,953.14	1362.94	67,186.30	N
15	50,000	1	25,487.11	133,176.94	2407.64	78,762.94	Y
16	50,000	2	6313.54	125,112.45	9515.98	116,294.24	Y
17	50,000	3	3744.60	196,970.08	6727.98	220,488.81	N
18	50,000	4	13,261.61	334,846.96	19,096.74	284,140.74	Y
19	50,000	5	4430.90	67,546.64	1606.70	57,256.59	Y
20	100,000	1	23,441.53	312,086.87	29,796.32	441,193.89	N
21	200,000	1	64,274.85	5,147,858.37	28,841.52	5,076,289.65	Y
250,000 with Bayes Opt			151,959.56	1,260,099.15	201,002.33	961,150.56	Y

The model outperformed in predicting claim ultimate amounts for 75% of the test cases with policy exposures of 10,000 or over, however, failed to achieve good results for the cases with 5000 policies, due to frequent failing to converge.

However, with neural networks being randomly initialised, there is significant variation in trained model predictions between training runs. We flag model reproducibility and stability as an issue to address for future research into neural based reserving approaches, with the observation that the random initialisations of training weights may lead to variations in the model predictions.

4.2. Bayesian Optimisation of Hyperparameters

The Bayesian optimisation of the hyperparameter set led to penalty factors of $l1$ and $l2$ of linear weights being 0.0103, $l2$ on the bias being 0.0048, and $l2$ on the dense network of 0.0003. This appears to have led to a good ultimate claim amount prediction, but claim count predictions performing slightly poorer on holdout data.

Although both claim count and claim paid were normalised to means of 1.0 prior to fitting, payments are more variable and consequently contribute a higher proportion of the total squared loss; so it is possible that having the same hyperparameters for both may have led to optimizing the fit of paid while neglecting count.

For the risk pricing applications, Table 3 shows a reasonable lift and also reasonable matching between modelled and actual payments.

Table 3. Model versus actual paid segmentation performance—250 k (closer is better).

Percentile	Model Paid	Actual Paid
5%	0.25	0.23
10.0%	0.33	0.32
15.0%	0.47	0.47
20.0%	0.6	0.38
25.0%	0.66	0.5
30.0%	0.71	0.54
35.0%	0.76	0.54
40.0%	0.8	0.51
45.0%	0.85	0.6
50.0%	0.9	0.67
55.0%	0.96	1.16
60.0%	1.02	1.24
65.0%	1.1	1.58
70.0%	1.18	1.18
75.0%	1.28	1.17
80.0%	1.39	0.96
85.0%	1.49	1.03
90.0%	1.62	1.8
95.0%	1.77	2.01
100.0%	2.24	3.06

This suggests the model is able to correctly distinguish higher and lower risk pricing factors within the portfolio.

With these hyperparameters, the weight attributed to the interpretable model compared to the neural model remained at 71% for claim count and 54% for claim paid, with the lack of weighting of the neural model suggesting that the simpler approach continued to be quite important despite the neural net components.

4.3. Regularisation

Table 4 shows the average absolute value of weights in the dense layers.

Table 4. Average absolute value of weights: dense layers.

Weight Decay (l2)	Paid w *	Dense Layer 1	Dense Layer 2	Dense Layer 3
0.0001	0.97	0.043	0.026	0.031
0.001	2.51	0.016	0.009	0.007
0.01	2.39	8.26×10^{-5}	1.57×10^{-5}	2.71×10^{-4}
0.1	0.64	0.004	2.36×10^{-5}	4.02×10^{-5}

* Weighting to residual model is $e^w/(1 + e^w)$.

A small amount of regularisation appears to be helpful to the fit of the residual model, increasing its weight, but as expected, as weight decay is increased towards higher values, the contribution of the neural network to the blended model diminishes. Due to random initialisation of the network for training, there is some variation in the results.

5. Extending with Freeform Data—Claim Description

There are a number of examples outside actuarial modelling that incorporate unstructured data into neural network models. Typically, this is done by using a pre-trained network for the type of data, such as VG-16G for images, Word2Vec for words, or BERT (Devlin et al. 2018) for sentences. The intermediate outputs of the pre-trained model are used as features for the main model.

However, we are not aware of any academic publications to date applying it within the domain of claims reserving. To demonstrate the earlier claims in Section 1.3, an example would be to extend the model to use freeform text incident descriptions. The incident description for each claim consists of a short phrase manually entered by claims staff describing the claim, e.g., 'insured damaged phone'. The code is available at: https://gist.github.com/JackyP/99141e403df720a2e752b9bbf08e428c.

The adjustments to the modelling process are as follows: the training dataset consists of the associated incident description and the corresponding subset of the policy-claims data from Section 3 that have had claims. Sentences are tokenised into integer vectors with each vector representing a word. Then, the pre-trained BERT network converts these vectors into an intermediate representation. These are then incorporated as additional features into an expanded model.

6. Conclusions

We extended the use of risk-pricing residual networks to granular reserving applications by introducing a claims development percentage sub-network with a softmax layer to produce a multi-task claim count and paid output, and found it had good performance benchmarked against a traditional PPCI approach when trained on sufficient dataset size.

In regards to interpretability, the softmax layer ensures claims development percentages sum to 100%, and consequently allows separation of risk pricing and claims development effects, whilst also jointly fitting them in a single model. In addition, we also introduced and discussed the concept of separate regularisation between linear and deep effects as a penalty on 'unexplainability'.

For practical application on large insurance datasets, we tested the use of Adam optimiser with learn rate search, "1cycle" policy optimisation, and setting of reasonable initial bias values. We found this led to effective results, and reasonable training times enabled Bayesian cross-validation optimisation algorithms to be accessible.

To demonstrate the flexible nature of neural networks, the model was also extended with a pre-trained BERT model to use the incident description as a freeform text input for predicting claim payments.

Overall while neural networks techniques for granular loss reserving remains nascent, we anticipate significant opportunities for it to continue developing in the future.

Funding: This research received no external funding.

Conflicts of Interest: The author declares no conflict of interest.

References

Devlin, Jacob, Ming-Wei Chang, Kenton Lee, and Kristina Toutanova. 2018. BERT: Pre-training of Bidirectional Transformers for Language Understanding. *arXiv*, arXiv:1810.04805.
Fotso, Stephane. 2018. Deep Neural Networks for Survival Analysis Based on a Multi-Task Framework. *arXiv*, arXiv:1801.05512v1.
He, Kaiming, Xiangyu Zhang, Shaoqing Ren, and Jian Sun. 2015. Deep Residual Learning for Image Recognition. *arXiv*, arXiv:1512.03385.
Kingma, Diederik, and Jimmy Ba. 2015. Adam: A Method for Stochastic Optimization. *arXiv*, arXiv:1412.6980.
Kuo, Kevin. 2018. DeepTriangle: A Deep Learning Approach to Loss Reserving. *arXiv*, arXiv:1804.09253v3.
Miller, Hugh, Gráinne McGuire, and Greg Taylor. 2016. Self-Assembling Insurance Claim models. Available online: https://actuaries.asn.au/Library/Events/GIS/2016/4dHughMillerSelfassemblingclaimmodels.pdf (accessed on 24 August 2019).
Poon, Jacky. 2018. Analytics Snippet: Multitasking Risk Pricing Using Deep Learning. Available online: https://www.actuaries.digital/2018/08/23/analytics-snippet-multitasking-risk-pricing-using-deep-learning (accessed on 13 June 2019).
Ribeiro, Marco Tulio, Sameer Singh, and Carlos Guestrin. 2016. "Why Should I Trust You?": Explaining the Predictions of Any Classifier. *arXiv*, arXiv:1602.04938v3.
Schelldorfer, Jürg, and Mario V. Wuthrich. 2019. Nesting Classical Actuarial Models into Neural Networks. Available online: https://ssrn.com/abstract=3320525 (accessed on 22 January 2019).
Semenovich, Dimitri, Ian Heppell, and Yang Cai. 2010. *Convex Models: A New Approach to Common Problems in Premium Rating*. Sydney: The Institute of Actuaries of Australia.
Smith, Leslie N. 2018. A disciplined approach to neural network hyper-parameters: Part 1—Learning rate, batch size, momentum, and weight decay. *arXiv*, arXiv:1803.09820v2.
Srivastava, Nitish, Geoffrey Hinton, Alex Krizhevsky, Ilya Sutskever, and Ruslan Salakhutdinov. 2014. Dropout: A Simple Way to Prevent Neural Networks from Overfitting. *The Journal of Machine Learning Research* 15: 1929–58.
Taylor, Greg, Gráinne McGuire, and James Sullivan. 2008. Individual claim loss reserving conditioned by case estimates. *Annals of Actuarial Science* 3: 215–56. [CrossRef]
Vaughan, Joel, Agus Sudjianto, Erind Brahimi, Jie Chen, and Vijayan N. 2018. Nair. Explainable Neural Networks based on Additive Index Models. *arXiv*, arXiv:1806.01933v1.

© 2019 by the author. Licensee MDPI, Basel, Switzerland. This article is an open access article distributed under the terms and conditions of the Creative Commons Attribution (CC BY) license (http://creativecommons.org/licenses/by/4.0/).

Article

Loss Reserving Models: Granular and Machine Learning Forms

Greg Taylor

School of Risk and Actuarial Studies, University of New South Wales, Kensington, NSW 2052, Australia; gregory.taylor@unsw.edu.au

Received: 10 May 2019; Accepted: 18 June 2019; Published: 19 July 2019

Abstract: The purpose of this paper is to survey recent developments in granular models and machine learning models for loss reserving, and to compare the two families with a view to assessment of their potential for future development. This is best understood against the context of the evolution of these models from their predecessors, and the early sections recount relevant archaeological vignettes from the history of loss reserving. However, the larger part of the paper is concerned with the granular models and machine learning models. Their relative merits are discussed, as are the factors governing the choice between them and the older, more primitive models. Concluding sections briefly consider the possible further development of these models in the future.

Keywords: granular models; loss reserving; machine learning; neural networks

1. Background

The history of loss reserving models, spanning 50-odd years, displays a general trend toward ever-increasing complexity and data-intensity. The objectives of this development have been broadly two-fold, both drawing on increased richness of the data. One objective has been increased predictive power; the other the enablement of modelling of the micro-mechanisms of the claim process (which may also enhance predictive power).

Two families of model that have undergone development within this context over the past decade are granular models (GMs) and machine learning models (MLMs). The first of these, also known as micro-models, is aimed at the second objective above. As the complexity of model structures increases, feature selection and parameter estimation also become more complex, time-consuming and expensive. MLMs are sometimes seen as a suitable means of redress of these difficulties.

The purpose of the present paper is to survey the history of loss reserving models, and how that history has led to the most recent types of model, granular forms and machine learning forms. History has not yet resolved whether one of these forms is superior to the other, or whether they can coexist in harmony. To some extent, therefore, they are currently in competition with each other.

Claim models may be developed for purposes other than loss reserving, with different imperatives. For example, pricing will require differentiation between individual risks, which loss reserving may or may not require. Here, emphasis will be placed on loss reserving applications throughout. The performance of the models considered here might be evaluated differently in relation to other applications.

Much of the historical development of loss reserving models has been, if not driven, at least enabled by the extraordinary increase in computing capacity that has occurred over the past 50 years or so. This has encouraged the analysis of more extensive data and the inclusion of more features in models.

Some of the resulting innovations have been of obvious benefit. However, the advantages and disadvantages of each historical model innovation will be discussed here, and this will create a perspective from which one may attempt to anticipate whether one of the two model forms is likely to gain ascendancy over the other in the near future.

Sections 3–6 proceed through the archaeology of loss reserving models. Archaeological ages are identified, marking fundamental breaks in model evolution. These sections proceed roughly chronologically, discussing many of the families of models contained in the literature, identifying their relative advantages and disadvantages.

These historical perspectives sharpen one's perspective on the issues associated with the more modern GMs and MLMs. They expose the strengths and weaknesses of earlier models, and place in focus those areas where the GMs and MLMs might have potential for improved methodology.

Against this background, Section 7 discusses the criteria for model selection, and Section 8 concentrates on the predictive efficiency of GMs and MLMs. Section 8 also discusses one or two aspects of MLMs that probably require resolution before those models will be widely accepted, and Sections 9 and 10 draw the discussion of the previous sections together to reach some conclusions and conjectures about the future.

It is not the purpose of this paper to provide a summary of an existing methodology. This is provided by various texts. The real purpose is set out in the preceding paragraph, and the discussion of historical model forms other than GMs or MLMs is introduced only to provide relevant context to the GM–MLM comparison.

Thus, a number of models will be introduced without, or with only brief, description. It is assumed that the reader is either familiar with the relevant detail or can obtain it from the cited reference.

2. Notation and Terminology

This paper will consider numerous models, with differing data requirements. The present section will establish a relatively general data framework that will serve for most of these models. All but the most modern of these are covered to some degree in the standard loss reserving texts, Taylor (1986, 2000) and Wüthrich and Merz (2008).

Claim data may relate to individual or aggregate claims, but will often be labelled by accident period and development period. These periods are not assumed to be years, but it is assumed that they are all of equal duration, e.g., accident quarter and development quarter. Other cases are possible, e.g., accident year and development quarter, but add to the notational complexity while adding little insight to the discussion.

Let $Y_{ij}^{[n]}$ denote claim payments in development period j in respect of claim n, which was incurred in accident period i. The couple (i, j) will be referred to as a cell. Also, define the total claim payments associated with the (i, j) cell as

$$Y_{ij} = \sum_n Y_{ij}^{[n]}$$

Usually, $Y_{ij}^{[n]}$ will be considered to be a random variable, and a realization of it will be denoted by $y_{ij}^{[n]}$. Likewise, a realisation of Y_{ij} will be denoted by y_{ij}. As a matter of notation, $E\left[Y_{ij}^{[n]}\right] = \mu_{ij}^{[n]}$, $Var\left[Y_{ij}^{[n]}\right] = \sigma_{ij}^{2[n]}$ and $E\left[Y_{ij}\right] = \mu_{ij}$, $Var\left[Y_{ij}\right] = \sigma_{ij}^2$.

Many simple claim models use the conventional data triangle, in which cells exist for $i = 1, 2, \ldots, I$ and $j = 1, 2, \ldots, I - i + 1$, which may be represented in triangular form with i and j indexing rows and columns, respectively, as illustrated in Figure 1.

It is useful to note at this early stage that the (i, j) cell falls on the $(i + j - 1)$-th diagonal of the triangle. Payments occurring anywhere along this diagonal are made in the same calendar period, and accordingly diagonals are referred to as calendar periods or payment periods.

It will be useful, for some purposes, to define cumulative claim payments. For claim n, from accident period i, the cumulative claim payments to the end of development period j are defined as

$$X_{ij}^{[n]} = \sum_{k=1}^{j} Y_{ik}^{[n]}$$

and the definition is extended in the obvious way to X_{ij}, the aggregate, for all claims incurred in accident period i, of cumulative claim payments to the end of development period j.

A quantity of interest later is the operational time (OT) at the finalisation of a claim. OT was introduced to the loss reserving literature by Reid (1978), and is discussed by Taylor (2000) and Taylor and McGuire (2016).

Let the OT for claim n be denoted $\tau^{[n]}$, defined as follows. Suppose that claim n belongs to accident period $i^{[n]}$, and that $\hat{N}_{i^{[n]}}$ is an estimator of the number of claims incurred in this accident period. Let $F^{[n]}_{i^{[n]}}$ denote the number of claims from the accident period finalised up to and including claim n. Then $\tau^{[n]} = F^{[n]}_{i^{[n]}} / \hat{N}_{i^{[n]}}$. In other words, $\tau^{[n]}$ is the proportion of claims from the same accident period as claim n that are finalised up to and including claim n.

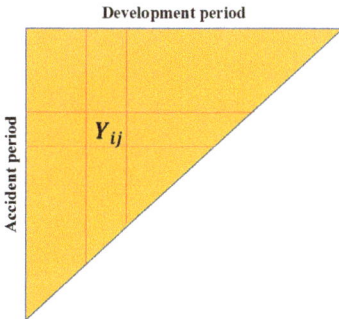

Figure 1. Illustration of the data triangle.

3. The Jurassic Period

The earliest models date generally from the late 1960s. These include the chain ladder and the separation method, and all their derivatives, such as Bornhuetter–Ferguson and Cape Cod. They are discussed in Taylor (1986, 2000) and Wüthrich and Merz (2008). The chain ladder's provenance seems unclear, but it may well have preceded the 1960s.

These models were based on the notion of "development" of an aggregate of claims over time, i.e., the tendency for the total payments made in respect of those claims to increase over time in accordance with some recognisable pattern. They therefore fall squarely in the class of phenomenological, or non-causal, models, in which attention is given to only mathematical patterns in the data rather than the mechanics of the claim process or any causal factors.

Figure 2 is a slightly enhanced version of Figure 1, illustrating the workings of the chain ladder. It is assumed that a cell (i, j) develops to its successor $(i, j+1)$ in accordance with the rule

$$x_{i,j+1} = f_j x_{ij}, \qquad (1)$$

where f_j is a parameter describing development, and referred to as a development factor or an age-to-age factor.

Forecasts are made according to this rule. The trick is to estimate factors f_j from past experience, and in practice they were typically estimated by some kind of averaging of past observations on these factors, i.e., observed values of $x_{i,j+1}/x_{ij}$.

Models of this type are very simple, but their most interesting quality is that they are not, in fact, models at all. The original versions of these models were not stochastic, as is apparent from (1). Nor is (1) even true over the totality of past experience; it is not the case for a typical data set that $x_{i,j+1}/x_{ij} = f_j$, constant for fixed j, but varying i. So, the "models" in this group are actually algorithms rather than models in the true sense.

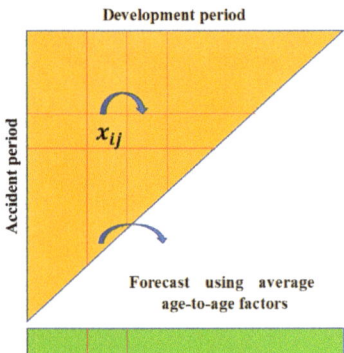

Figure 2. Illustration of a forecast by age-to-age factors.

Of course, this fault has been rectified over the subsequent years, with (1) replaced by the genuine model defined by the following conditions:

(a) Each row of the triangle is a Markov chain.
(b) Distinct rows of the triangle are stochastically independent.
(c) $X_{i,j+1}|X_{ij}$ is subject to some defined distribution for which $E[X_{i,j+1}|X_{ij}] = f_j X_{ij}$, where f_j is a parameter to be estimated from data.

A model of this sort was proposed by Mack (1993) ("the Mack model"), and much development of it has followed, though the earliest stochastic formulation of the chain ladder (Hachemeister and Stanard 1975) should also be credited.

While the formulation of a genuine chain ladder model was immensely useful, the fundamental structure of the model retains some shortcomings. First, in statistical parlance, it is a multiplicative row-and-column effect model. This is a very simple structure, in which all rows are just, in expectation, scalar multiples of one another. This lacks the complexity to match much real-life claim experience.

For example, a diagonal effect might be present, e.g., $E[X_{i,j+1}|X_{ij}] = f_j g_{i+j-1} X_{ij}$, in (c), where g_{i+j-1} is a parameter specific to diagonal $i + j - 1$. A variable inflationary effect would appear in this form, but cannot be accommodated in the chain ladder model formulated immediately above. One can add such parameters to the model, but this will exacerbate the over-parameterisation problem described in the next main dot point.

Rates of claim settlement might vary from one row to another, causing variation in the factors f_j (Fisher and Lange 1973). Again, one can include additional effects in the models, but at the expense of additional parameters.

Second, even with this simple form, it is at risk of over-parameterisation. The model of an $n \times n$ triangle and the associated forecast are characterised by $2(n-1)$ parameters, $f_1, \ldots, f_{I-1}, Y_{2,I-1}, X_{3,I-2}, \ldots, X_{I1}$ (actually, the last $n-1$ of these are conditioning observations but function essentially as parameters in the forecast). For example, a 10×10 triangle would contain 55 observations, would forecast 45 cells, and would require 18 parameters. Over-parameterisation can increase forecast error.

The Jurassic continued through the 1970s and into the 1980s, during which time it spawned mainly non-stochastic models. It did, however, produce some notably advanced creatures. Hachemeister and Stanard (1975) has already been mentioned. A stochastic model of claim development essentially by curve fitting was introduced by Reid (1978), and Hachemeister (1978, 1980) constructed a stochastic model of individual claim development.

4. The Cretaceous Period—Seed-Bearing Organisms Appear

The so-called models of the Jurassic period assumed the general form:

$$Y_{ij} = g(Y, \alpha) \tag{2}$$

where g is some real-valued function, Y is the vector containing the entire set of observations as its components, and α is some set of parameters, either exogenous or estimated from Y. The case of the chain ladder represented by (1) is an example in which $\alpha = \{f_1, \ldots, f_{I-1}\}$.

Although (2) is not a stochastic model, it may be converted to one by the simple addition of a stochastic error ε_{ij}:

$$Y_{ij} = g(Y, \alpha) + \varepsilon_{ij}, E[\varepsilon_{ij}] = 0 \tag{3}$$

Note that the Mack model of Section 3 is an example. In addition, with some limitation of g and ε_{ij}, (3) becomes a Generalised Linear Model (GLM) (McCullagh and Nelder 1989), specified as follows:

(a) $Y_{ij} \sim F(\mu_{ij}, \varphi/w_{ij})$ where $\mu_{ij} = E[Y_{ij}]$ and F is a distribution contained in the exponential dispersion family (EDF) (Nelder and Wedderburn 1972) with dispersion parameter φ and weights w_{ij};

(b) μ_{ij} takes the parametric form $h(\mu_{ij}) = x_{ij}^T \beta$ for some one–one function h (called the link function), and where x_{ij} is a vector of covariates associated with the (i, j) cell and β the corresponding parameter vector.

Again, the chain ladder provides an example. The choices $h = \ln$, $x_{i,j+1}^T = [0, \ldots 0, X_{i,j}, 0 \ldots 0]$, $\beta = [f_1, f_2, \ldots]^T$ yield the Mack model of Section 3.

The Cretaceous period consisted of such models. The history of actuarial GLMs is longer than is sometimes realised. Its chronology is as follows:

- in 1972, the concept was introduced by Nelder and Wedderburn;
- in 1977, modelling software called GLIM was introduced;
- in 1984, the Tweedie family of distributions was introduced (Tweedie 1984), simplifying the modelling software;
- in 1990 and later, seminal actuarial papers (Wright 1990; Brockman and Wright 1992) appeared.

GLMs were not widely used in an actuarial context until 1990, and to some extent this reflected the limitations of earlier years' computing power. It should be noted that their actuarial introduction to domestic lines pricing occurred as early as 1979 (Baxter et al. 1980). I might be permitted to add here a personal note that they were heavily used for loss reserving in all the consultancies with which I was associated from the early 1980s.

The range of GLM loss reserving applications has expanded considerably since 1990. A few examples are:

- analysis of an Auto Liability (relatively long-tailed) portfolio (Taylor and McGuire 2004) with:
    - rates of claim settlement that varied over time;
    - superimposed inflation (SI) (a diagonal effect) that varied dramatically over time and also over OT (defined in Section 2);
    - a change of legislation affecting claim sizes (a row effect);
- analysis of a mortgage insurance portfolio (Taylor and Mulquiney 2007), using a cascade of GLM sub-models of experience in different policy states, viz.
    - healthy policies;

- policies in arrears;
  - policies in respect of properties that have been taken into possession; and
  - policies in respect of which claims have been submitted;
- analysis of a medical malpractice portfolio (Taylor et al. 2008), modelling the development of individual claims, both payments and case reserves, taking account of a number of claim covariates, such as medical specialty and geographic area of practice; and
- a monograph on GLM reserving (Taylor and McGuire 2016).

It is of note that chain ladder model structures may be regarded as special cases of the GLM. Indeed, these chain ladder formulations may be found in the literature (Taylor 2011; Taylor and McGuire 2016; Wüthrich and Merz 2008). However, these form a small subset of all GLM claim models.

5. The Paleogene—Increased Diversity in the Higher Forms

5.1. Adaptation of Species—Evolutionary Models

Recall the general form of GLM set out in Section 4, and note that the parameter vector β is constant over time. It is possible, of course, that it might change.

Consider, for example, the Mack model of Section 3. One might wish to adopt such a model but with parameters $f_1, \ldots, f_{I-1}$ varying stochastically from one row to the next. This type of modelling can be achieved by a simple extension of the GLM framework defined in Section 4. The resulting model is the following.

Evolutionary (or adaptive) GLM. For brevity here, adopt the notation $t = i + j - 1$, so that t indexes payment period. Let the observations Y_{ij} satisfy the conditions:

(a) $Y_{ij} \sim F\left(\mu_{ij}^{(t)}, \varphi/w_{ij}\right)$ where $\mu_{ij}^{(t)} = E[Y_{ij}]$;

(b) $\mu_{ij}^{(t)}$ takes the parametric form $h\left(\mu_{ij}^{(t)}\right) = x_{ij}^T \beta^{(t)}$, where the parameter vector is now $\beta^{(t)}$ in payment period t; and

(c) The vector $\beta^{(t)}$ is now random: $\beta^{(t)} \sim P\left(.; \beta^{(t-1)}, \psi\right)$, which is a distribution that is a natural conjugate of $F(.,.)$ with its own dispersion parameter ψ.

If this is compared with the static GLM of Section 4, then the earlier model can be seen to have been adjusted in the following ways:

- all parameters have been superscripted with a time index;
- the fundamental parameter vector $\beta^{(t)}$ is now randomised, with a prior distribution that is conditioned by $\beta^{(t-1)}$, the parameter vector at the preceding epoch.

The model parameters evolve thus through time, allowing for the model to adapt to changing data trends. A specific example of the evolution (c) would be a stationary random walk in which $\beta^{(t)} = \beta^{(t-1)} + \eta^{(t)}$ with $\eta^{(t)} \sim P^*(.; \psi)$, with P^* now a prior on $\eta^{(t)}$ and subject to $E\left[\eta^{(t)}\right] = 0$.

The mathematics of evolutionary models were investigated by Taylor (2008) and numerical applications given by Taylor and McGuire (2009). Their structure is reminiscent of the Kalman filter (Harvey 1989) but with the following important difference that the Kalman filter is the evolutionary form of a general linear model, whereas the model described here is the evolutionary form of a GLM.

Specifically,

- the Kalman filter requires a linear relation between observation means and parameter vectors, whereas the present model admits nonlinearity through the link function;
- the Kalman filter requires Gaussian error terms in respect of both observations and priors, whereas the present model admits non-Gaussian within the EDF.

One difficulty arising within this type of model is that the admission of nonlinearity often causes the posterior of $\beta^{(t)}$ in (c) to lie outside the family of conjugate priors of F at the next step of the evolution, where $\beta^{(t)}$ evolves to $\beta^{(t+1)}$. This adds greatly to the complexity of its implementation.

The references cited earlier (Taylor 2008; Taylor and McGuire 2009) proceed by replacing the posterior for $\beta^{(t)}$, which forms the prior for $\beta^{(t+1)}$, by the natural conjugate of F that has the same mean and covariance structure as the actual posterior. This is reported to work reasonably well, though with occasional stability problems in the conversion of iterates to parameter estimates.

5.2. Miniaturisation of Species—Parameter Reduction

The Jurassic models were lumbering, with overblown parameter sets. The GLMs of Section 4 were more efficient in limiting the size of the parameter set, but without much systematic attention to the issue. A more recent approach that brings the issue into focus is regularised regression, and specifically the least absolute shrinkage and selection operator (LASSO) model (Tibshirani 1996).

Consider the GLM defined by (a) and (4) in Section 4. At this point, let the data set be quite general in form. It might consist of the Y_{ij}, as in (3); or of the $Y_{ij}^{[n]}$ defined in Section 2; or, indeed, of any other observations capable of forming the independent variable of a GLM. Let this general data set be denoted by $\mathcal{Y}$.

The parameter vector β of the GLM is typically estimated by maximum likelihood estimation. For this purpose, the negative log-likelihood (actually, negative log-quasi-likelihood) of the observations $\mathcal{Y}$ given β is calculated. This is otherwise known as the scaled deviance, and will be denoted $D(\mathcal{Y};\beta)$. The estimate of β is then

$$\hat{\beta} = \underset{\beta}{\operatorname{argmin}} D(\mathcal{Y};\beta). \tag{4}$$

Here, the deviance operates as a loss function. Consider the following extension of this loss function:

$$L(\mathcal{Y};\beta) = D(\mathcal{Y};\beta) + \lambda \|\beta\|_p \tag{5}$$

where $\|\ \|_p$ denotes the L_p norm and $\lambda > 0$ is a constant, to be discussed further below.

This inclusion of the additional member in (5) converts the earlier GLM to a regularised GLM. In parallel with (4), its estimate of β is

$$\hat{\beta} = \underset{\beta}{\operatorname{argmin}} L(\mathcal{Y};\beta). \tag{6}$$

Certain special cases of regularised regression are common in the literature, as summarised in Table 1.

Table 1. Special cases of regularised regression.

λ	p	Special Case
0	-	GLM
>0	1	Lasso
>0	2	Ridge regression

The case of particular interest here is the lasso. According to (5), the loss function is

$$L(\mathcal{Y};\beta) = D(\mathcal{Y};\beta) + \lambda \|\beta\|_1 = D(\mathcal{Y};\beta) + \lambda \sum_k |\beta_k| \tag{7}$$

where the β_k are the components of β.

A property of this form of loss function is that it can force many components of $\hat{\beta}$ to zero, rendering the lasso an effective tool for elimination of covariates from a large set of candidates.

The term $\lambda\|\beta\|_1$ in (7) may be viewed as a penalty for every parameter included in the model. Evidently, the penalty increases with increasing λ, with the two extreme cases recognisable:

- $\lambda \to 0$: no elimination of covariates (ordinary GLM—see also Table 1);
- $\lambda \to \infty$: elimination of all covariates (trivial regression).

Thus, the application of the lasso may consist of defining a GLM in terms of a very large number of candidate covariates, and then calibrating by means of the lasso, which has the effect of selecting a subset of these candidates for inclusion in the model.

The prediction accuracy of any model produced by the lasso is evaluated by cross-validation, which consists of the following steps:

(a) Randomly delete one n-th of the data set, as a test sample;
(b) Fit the model to the remainder of the data set (the training set);
(c) Generate fitted values for the test sample;
(d) Compute a defined measure of error (e.g., the sum of squared differences) between the test sample and the values fitted to it;
(e) Repeat steps (a) to (d) a large number of times, and take the average of the error measures, calling this the cross-validation error (CV error).

The process just described pre-supposes a data set sufficiently large for dissection into a training set and a test sample. Small claim triangles (e.g., a 10 × 10 triangle contains only 55 observations) are not adapted to this. So, cross-validation is a model performance measure suited to large data sets, such as are analysed by GMs and MLMs.

One possible form of calibration (e.g., McGuire et al. (2018)) proceeds as follows. A sequence of models is examined with increasing λ, and therefore with the number of covariates decreasing. The models with small λ tend to be over-parameterised, leading to poor predictive performance; those with large λ tend to be under-parameterised, again leading to poor predictive performance. The optimal model is chosen to minimise CV error.

It is evident that, by the nature of this calibration, the lasso will be expected to lead to high forecast efficiency.

Figure 3 provides a numerical example of the variation of CV error with the number of parameters used to model a particular data set.

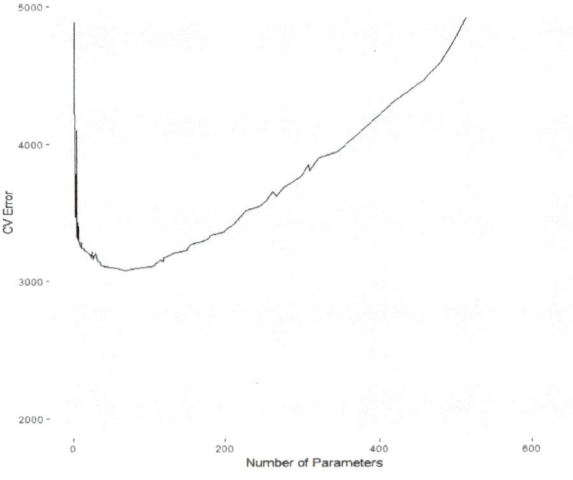

Figure 3. An example of cross-validation error.

The lasso is a relatively recent addition to the actuarial literature, but a number of applications have already been made. Li et al. (2017) and Venter and Şahın (2018) used it to model mortality. Gao and Meng (2018) constructed a loss reserving lasso, modelling a 10 × 10 aggregate claim triangle and using a model broadly related to the chain ladder. McGuire et al. (2018) also constructed a loss reserving lasso, but modelling a large data set of individual claims containing a number of complex data features, some of which will be described in Section 6.

5.3. Granular (or Micro-) Models

Granular models, sometimes referred to as micro-models, are not especially well-defined. The general idea is that they endeavour to extend modelling into some of the detail that underlies the aggregate data in a claim triangle. For example, a granular model may endeavour to model individual claims in terms of the detail of the claim process.

Hachemeister's (1978, 1980) individual claim model has already been mentioned. The early statistical case estimation models used in industry were also granular. See, for example, Taylor and Campbell (2002) for a model of workers compensation claims in which claimants move between "active" and "incapacitated" states, receiving benefits for incapacity and other associated benefits, such as medical costs.

The history of granular models is generally regarded as having commenced with the papers of Norberg (1993, 1999) and Hesselager (1994). These authors represented individual claims by a model that tracked a claim process through a sequence of key dates, namely accident date, notification date, partial payment date, ... , partial payment date, final payment date, and closure date. The process is a marked process in the sense that each payment date is tagged with a payment amount (or mark).

This type of model has been implemented by Pigeon et al. (2013, 2014) and Antonio and Plat (2014). Comment will be made on the performance of these models in Section 8.2.

Distinction is sometimes made between aggregate and granular models, but it is debatable. The literature contains models with more extensive data inputs than just claim payment triangles. For example, the payment triangle might be supplemented by a claim count triangle, as in the Payments per Claim Incurred model described in Taylor (2000), or in the Double Chain Ladder of Miranda et al. (2013).

These models certainly use more extensive data than a simple claim amount triangle, but the data are still aggregated. It is more appropriate to regard claim models as forming a spectrum that varies from a small amount of conditioning data at one end (e.g., a chain ladder) to a very large amount at the other (e.g., the individual claim models of Pigeon, Antonio and Denuit).

6. The Anthropocene—Intelligent Beings Intervene

6.1. Artificial Neural Networks in General

By implication, the present section will be concerned with the application of machine learning (ML) to loss reserving. Once again, the classification of specific models as MLMs or not may be ambiguous. If ML is regarded as algorithmic investigation of patterns and structure in data with minimal human intervention, then the lasso of Section 5.2 might be regarded as an MLM.

There are other contenders, such as regression trees, random forests, support vector machines, and clustering (Wüthrich and Buser 2017), but the form of ML that has found greatest application to loss reserving is the artificial neural network (ANN), and this section will concentrate on these.

Just a brief word on the architecture of a (feed-forward) ANN, since it will be relevant to the discussion in Section 8.3. Using the notation of Kuo (2018), let the ANN input be a vector x. Suppose there are $L-1$ (≥ 1) hidden layers of neurons, each layer a vector, with values denoted by $h^{[1]}, \ldots, h^{[L-1]}$; a vector output layer, with a value denoted by $h^{[L]}$; and a vector prediction $\hat{y}$ of some target quantity y. Let the components of $h^{[\ell]}$ be denoted by $h^{[\ell]}_j$.

The relevant computational relations are

$$h_j^{[\ell]} = g^{[\ell]}\left(z_j^{[\ell]}\right), \ell = 1, 2, \ldots, L \tag{8}$$

$$z^{[\ell]} = \left(w^{[\ell]}\right)^T \left(h^{[\ell-1]}\right) + b^{[\ell]}, \ell = 1, 2, \ldots, L \text{ with the convention } h^{[0]} = x \tag{9}$$

$$\hat{y} = h^{[L]} \tag{10}$$

where $z^{[\ell]}$ is a vector with components $z_j^{[\ell]}$, the $g^{[\ell]}$ are prescribed activation functions, the $h_j^{[\ell]}$ are called activations, $w^{[\ell]}$ is a vector of weights, and $b^{[\ell]}$ is a vector of biases. The weights and biases are selected by the ANN to maximise the accuracy of the prediction.

The hidden layers need not be of equal length. The activation functions will usually be nonlinear.

An early application of an ANN was given by Mulquiney (2006), who modelled an earlier version of the data set used by McGuire et al. (2018) in Section 5.2. This consisted of a unit record file in respect of about 60,000 Auto Bodily Injury finalised claims, each tagged with its accident quarter, development quarter of finalisation, calendar quarter of finalisation, OT at finalisation and season of finalisation (quarter).

Prior GLM analysis of the data set over an extended period had been carried out by Taylor and McGuire (2004), as described in Section 4, and they found that claim costs were affected in a complex manner by the factors listed there. The ANN was able to identify these effects. For example, it identified:

- an accident quarter effect corresponding to the legislative change that occurred in the midst of the data; and
- SI that varied with both finalisation quarter and OT.

Although the ANN and GLM produced similar models, the ANN's goodness-of-fit was somewhat superior to that of the GLM.

Interest in and experimentation with ANNs has accelerated in recent years. Harej et al. (2017) reported on an International Actuarial Association Working Group on individual claim development with machine learning. Their model was a somewhat "under-powered" ANN that assumed separate chain ladder models for paid and incurred costs, respectively, for individual claims, and simply estimated the age-to-age factors.

However, since both paid and incurred amounts were included as input information in both models, they managed to differentiate age-to-age factors for different claims, e.g., claims with small amounts paid but large amounts incurred showed higher development of payments.

A follow-up study, with a similar restriction of ANN form, namely pre-supposed chain ladder structure, was published by Jamal et al. (2018).

Kuo (2018) carried out reserving with deep learning ANN, i.e., with multiple hidden layers. In this case, no model structure was pre-supposed. The ANN was applied to 200 claim triangles (50 insurers, each four lines of business) by Meyers and Shi (2011), and its results compared with those generated by five other models, including chain ladder and several from Meyers (2015).

The ANN out-performed all contenders most of the time and, in other cases, was only slightly inferior to them. This is an encouraging demonstration of the power of the ANN, but the small triangles of aggregate data do not exploit the potential of the ANN, which can be expected to perform well on large data sets that conceal complex structures.

The pace of development has picked up over the past couple of years. Wüthrich (2018a, 2018b) has been active. Other contributions include Ahlgren (2018) and Gabrielli (2019).

6.2. The Interpretability Problem

GMs and MLMs can greatly improve modelling power in cases of data containing complex patterns. GMs can delve deeply into the data and provide valuable detail of the claim process. Their formulation can, however, be subject to great, even unsurmountable, difficulties. MLMs, on the other hand, for the large part provide little understanding, but may be able to bypass the difficulties encountered by GMs. They may also be cost-effective in shifting modelling effort from the actuary to the algorithm (e.g., lasso).

MLMs' greatest obstacle to useful implementation is the interpretability problem. Some recent applications of ANNs have sought to address this. For example, Vaughan et al. (2018) introduce their explainable neural network (xNN), in which the ANN architecture (8) to (10) is restricted in such a way that

$$\hat{y} = \mu + \sum_{k=1}^{K} \gamma_k f_k(\beta_k^T x)$$

for scalar constants $\mu, \gamma_1, \ldots, \gamma_K$, vector constants $\beta_1, \ldots, \beta_K$, and real-valued functions f_k.

This formulation is an attempt to bring known structure to the prediction $\hat{y}$. It is similar to the use of basis functions in the lasso implementation of McGuire et al. (2018). The use of xNNs is as yet in its infancy but offers promise.

7. Model Assessment

The assessment of a specific loss reserving model needs to consider two main factors:

- the model's predictive efficiency; and
- its fitness for purpose.

7.1. Adaptation of Species—Evolutionary Models

Let R denote the quantum of total liability represented by the loss reserve, and $\hat{R}$ the statistical estimate of it. Both quantities are viewed as random variables, and the forecast error is $R - \hat{R}$, also a random variable.

Loss reserving requires some knowledge of the statistical properties of $\hat{R}$. Obviously, the mean $E[\hat{R}]$ is required as the central estimate. Depending on the purpose of the reserving exercise, one may also require certain quantiles of $\hat{R}$ for the establishment of risk margins and/or capital margins, but an important statistic will be the estimate of forecast error.

One such estimate is the mean square error of prediction (MSEP), defined as

$$MSEP[R - \hat{R}] = E[R - \hat{R}]^2. \tag{11}$$

The smaller the MSEP, the greater the predictive efficiency of $\hat{R}$, so a reasonable choice of model would often be that which minimises the MSEP (maximises prediction efficiency). As long as one is not concerned with quantiles other than moderate, e.g., 75%, this conclusion will hold. If there is a major focus on extreme quantiles, e.g., 99%, the criterion for model selection might shift to the tail properties of the distribution of $\hat{R}$.

It may often be assumed that $\hat{R}$ is unbiased, i.e., $E[R - \hat{R}] = 0$, but (11) may remain a reasonable measure of forecast error in the absence of this condition.

The structure of MSEP is discussed at some length in Taylor (2000, sec. 6.6) and Taylor and McGuire (2016, chp. 4). Suffice to say here that it consists of three additive components, identified as:

- parameter error;
- process error; and
- model error.

As discussed in the cited references, model error is often problematic and, for the purpose of the present subsection, MSEP will be taken to be the sum of just parameter and process errors.

In one or two cases, MSEP may be obtained analytically, most notably in the case of the Mack model, as set out in detail in Mack (1993). The MSEP of a GLM forecast may be approximated by the delta method, discussed in Taylor and McGuire (2016, sec. 5.2).

However, generally, for non-approximative estimates, two methods are available, namely:

- the bootstrap (Taylor and McGuire 2016, sec. 5.3); and
- (in the case of Bayesian models) Markov Chain Monte Carlo (MCMC) (Meyers 2015).

7.2. Fitness for Purpose

In certain circumstances, forecasts of ultimate claim cost may be required at an individual level. Suppose, for example, a self-insurer adopts a system of devolving claim cost to cost centres, but has not the wherewithal to formulate physical estimates of those costs. Then, a GM or MLM at the level of individual claims will be required.

If a loss reserving model is required not only for the simple purpose of entering a loss reserve in a corporate account, but also to provide some understanding of the claims experience that might be helpful to operations, then a more elaborate model than the simplest, such as chain ladder, would be justified.

Such considerations will determine the subset of all available models that are fit for purpose. Within this subset, one would, in principle, still usually choose that with the maximum predictive efficiency.

8. Predictive Efficiency

The purpose of the present section is to consider the predictive efficiency of GMs and MLMs. It will be helpful to preface this discussion with a discussion of cascaded models.

8.1. Cascaded Models

A cascaded model consists of a number of sub-models with the output of at least one of these providing input to another. An example is the Payments per Claim Finalized model discussed by Taylor (2000). This consists of three sub-models, as follows:

- claim notification counts;
- claim finalisation counts; and
- claim finalisation amounts.

The sub-models are configured as in Figure 4.

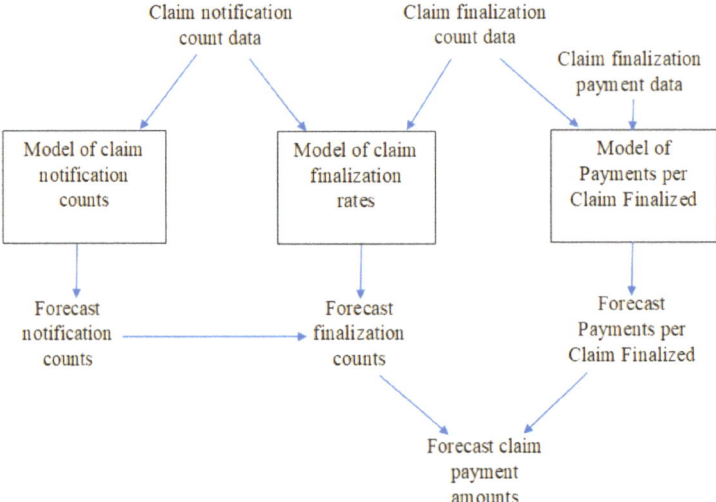

Figure 4. The Payments per Claim Finalized model and its sub-models.

By contrast, the chain ladder consists of just a single model of claim amounts.

It is evident that increasing the number of sub-models within a model must add to the number of parameters, and it is well-known that, although too few parameters will lead to a poor model due to bias in forecasts, an increase in the number of parameters beyond a certain threshold will lead to poor predictive efficiency (over-parameterisation).

A cascaded model of n sub-models would typically generate less biased forecasts than one of $n-1$ sub-models. However, the increased number of parameters might degrade predictive efficiency to the point where the more parsimonious model, even with its increased bias, is to be preferred.

It follows that the addition of a further sub-model will be justified only if the bias arising from its exclusion is sufficiently severe. This is illustrated in the empirical study by Taylor and Xu (2016) of many triangles from the data set of Meyers and Shi (2011).

They find that many of them are consistent with the assumptions of the chain ladder, in which case that model out-performs more elaborate cascaded models. However, there are also cases in which the chain ladder is a poor representation of the data, calling for a more elaborate model. In such cases, the cascaded models produce the superior performance.

8.2. Granular Models

The discussion of Section 8.1 perhaps sounds a cautionary note in relation to GMs. These are, by their nature, cascaded, e.g., a sub-model for the notification process, a sub-model for the partial payment process, etc. They may, in fact, be very elaborate, in which case the possibility of over-parameterisation becomes a concern.

A salutary remark in the consideration of GMs is that the (aggregate) chain ladder has minimum variance for over-dispersed Poisson observations (Taylor 2011). So, regardless of how one expands the scope of the input data (e.g., more precise accident and notification dates, individual claim data, etc.), the forecast of future claim counts will not be improved as long as the chain ladder assumptions are valid.

The GM literature is rather bereft of demonstration that a GM has out-performed less elaborate contenders. It is true that Huang et al. (2016) make this claim in relation to the data considered by them. However, a closer inspection reveals that their GM is essentially none other than the Payments per Claim Finalized model discussed in Section 8.1.

The model posits individual claim data, and generates individual claim loss reserves. However, the parameters controlling these individual reserves are not individual-claim-specific. So, the model appears to lie somewhere between an individual claim model and an aggregate model.

This does not appear to be a case of a GM producing predictive efficiency superior to that of an aggregate model. Rather, it is a case of a cascaded model producing efficiency superior to that of uncascaded models.

There is one other major characteristic of GMs that requires consideration. A couple of examples illustrate.

Example 1. *Recall Antonio and Plat (2014), whose model is of the type mentioned in Section 5.3, tracing individual claims through the process of occurrence, notification, partial payments and closure. Claim payments occur according to a distribution of delays from notification but, conditional on these, the severities of individual payments in respect of an individual claim are equi-distributed and stochastically independent.*

In some lines of business, perhaps most but especially in Liability lines, this assumption will not withstand scrutiny. The payments of a medium-to-large claim typically tend to resemble the following profile: a series of relatively small payments (fees for incident reports, preliminary medical expenses), a payment of dominant size (settlement of agreed liability), followed possibly by a smaller final payment (completion of legal expenses).

Consequently, if a large payment (say $500 K) is made, the probability of another of anywhere near the same magnitude is remote. In other words, the model requires recognition of dependency between payments.

Example 2. *(From Taylor et al. (2008)).* Consider a GM of development of case estimates over time. Suppose an estimate of ultimate liability in respect of an individual claim increases 10-fold, from $5 K to $50 K, over a particular period. Then, typically, the probability of a further 10-fold increase, from $50 K to $500 K, in the next period will be low.

The reason is that the first increase signifies the emergence of information critical to the quantum of the claim, and it is unusual that further information of the same importance would emerge separately in the following period. Again, the random variables describing the development of a claim cannot be assumed to be stochastically independent.

Taylor et al. (2008) suggest an estimation procedure that allows for any such dependency without the need for its explicit measurement.

The essential point to emerge from this discussion is that the detail of a claim process usually involves a number of intricate dependencies. One ignores these at one's peril, but taking account of them may well be problematic, since it opens the way to a hideously complex model with many dependency parameters. This, in turn, raises the spectre of over-parameterisation, and its attendant degradation of predictive efficiency, not to mention possible difficulty in the estimation of the dependency parameters.

This by no means condemns GMs, but it appears to me that the jury is still out on them; they have yet to prove their case.

8.3. Artificial Neural Networks

ANNs are effective tools for taking account of obscure or complex data structures. Recall the data set used by Mulquiney's (2006) ANN in Section 6, which had been previously modelled with a GLM. It is evident from the description of the results that the GLM would have required a number of interactions:

- for the legislative effect, interaction between accident quarter and OT;
- for SI, interaction between finalisation quarter and OT.

The seeking out of such effects in GLM modelling (feature selection) can be difficult, time-consuming and expensive. This point is made by McGuire et al. (2018) in favour of the lasso, which is intended to automate feature selection.

The ANN is an alternative form of automation. As can be seen from the model form set out in (8) to (10), no explicit feature selection is attempted. The modelling is essentially an exercise in nonlinear curve-fitting, the nonlinearity arising from the activation functions. The number of parameters in the model can be controlled by cross-validation, as described in Section 5.2.

To some extent ANNs provide a rejoinder to the dependency issues raised in Section 8.2. Identification of dependencies becomes a mere special case of feature selection, and is captured obscurely by (8) to (10).

On the other hand, the abstract curve-fitting nature of ANNs renders them dangerously susceptible to extrapolation errors. Consider SI, for example. In the forecast of a loss reserve, one needs to make some assumption for the future. A GLM will have estimated past SI, and while this might not be blindly extrapolated into the future, it can provide valuable information, perhaps to be merged with collateral information, leading to a reasoned forecast.

In the case of an ANN, any past SI will have been "modelled" in the sense that the model may include one or more functions that vary over calendar quarter, but these curves may interact with other covariates, as mentioned above, and the extraction of all this information in an organised and comprehensible form may present difficulties. Mulquiney (2006) alludes to this issue.

All actuaries are familiar with text-book examples of curves (e.g., polynomials) that fit well to past data points, but produce wild extrapolations into the future. Blind extrapolation of ANNs can, on occasion, produce such howlers. Suffice to say that care and, possibly, skill is required in their use for forecasting.

9. The Watchmaker and the Oracle

The tendency of GMs (watchmaking) is to increase the number of cascaded models (relative to aggregate models), first to individual claim modelling, then perhaps to individual transaction modelling, to dissect the available data in ever greater detail, to increase the number of model components and the complexity of their connections, and then assemble an integrated model from all the tiny parts.

If this can be achieved, it will provide powerful understanding of the claim process in question. However, as indicated in Section 8.2, the process is fraught with difficulty. The final model may be over-simplified and over-parameterised, with unfavourable implications for predictive efficiency. In addition, the issue of modelling complex stochastic dependencies may be difficult, or even impossible, to surmount.

One may even discover that all sub-models pass goodness-of-fit tests, and yet the integrated model, when assembled, does not. This can arise because of inappropriate connections between the sub-models or overlooked dependencies.

An example of this can occur in the workers compensation framework mentioned in Section 5.3. One might successfully model persistence in the active state as a survival process, and persistence in the incapacitated state as a separate survival process, and then combine the two to forecast a worker's future incapacity experience.

However, the active survival intensities may not be independent of the worker's history. A claim recently recovered from incapacity may be less likely to return to it over the following few days than a worker who has never been incapacitated. Failure to allow for this dependency (and possibly other similar ones) will lead to unrealistic forecasts of future experience.

The behaviour of the ANN is Oracle-like. It is presented with a question. It surveys the available information, taking account of all its complexities, and delivers an answer, with little trace of reasoning.

It confers the benefit of bypassing many of the challenges of granular modelling, but the price to be paid for this is an opaque model. This is the interpretability problem. Individual data features remain hidden within the model. They may also be sometimes poorly measured without the human assistance given to more structured models. For example, diagonal effects might be inaccurately measured, but compensated for by measured, but actually nonexistent, row effects. Similar criticisms can be levelled at some other MLMs, e.g., lasso.

The ANN might be difficult to validate. Cross-validation might ensure a suitably small MSEP overall. However, if a poor fit is found in relation to some subset of the data, one's recourse is unclear. The abstract nature of the model does not lend itself easily to spot-correction.

10. Conclusions

Aggregate models have a long track record. They are demonstrably adequate in some situations, and dubious to unsuitable in others. Cases may easily be identified in which a model as simple as the chain ladder works perfectly, and no other approach is likely to improve forecasting with respect to either bias or precision.

However, these simple models are characterised by very simple assumptions and, when a data set does not conform to these assumptions, the performance of the simple models may be seriously disrupted. Archetypal deviations from the simple model structures are the existence of variable SI, structural breaks in the sequence of average claim sizes over accident periods, or variable claim settlement rates (see e.g., Section 4).

When disturbances of this sort occur, great flexibility in model structure may be required. For a few decades, GLMs have provided this (see Section 4). GLMs continue to be applicable and useful. However, the fitting of these models requires considerable time and skill, and is therefore laborious and costly.

One possible response to this is the use of regularised regression, and the lasso in particular (Section 5.2). This latter model may be viewed as a form of MLM in that it automates model selection. This retains all the advantages of a GLM's flexibility, but with the reduced time and cost of calibration flowing from automation, and also provides a powerful guard against over-parameterisation.

The GMs of Section 5.3 are not a competitor of the GLM. Rather, they attempt to deconstruct the claim process into a number of components and model each of these. GLMs may well be used for the component modelling.

This approach may extract valuable information about the claim process that would otherwise be unavailable. However, as pointed out in Section 8.2, there will often be considerable difficulty in modelling some dependencies in the data, and failure to do so may be calamitous for predictive accuracy.

Most GMs are also cascaded models and, indeed, some are extreme cases of these. Section 8.1 points out that the complexity of cascaded models, largely reflected in the number of sub-models, comes with a cost in terms of enlarged predictive error (MSEP). They are therefore useful only when the failure to consider sub-models would cause the introduction of prediction bias worse than the increase in prediction error caused by their inclusion.

The increased computing power of recent years has enabled the recruitment of larger data sets, with a greater number of explanatory variables for loss reserving, or lower-level, such as individual claim, data. This can create difficulties for GMs and GLMs. The greater volume of data may suggest greater model complexity. It may, for example, necessitate an increase in the number of sub-models within a GLM.

If a manually constructed GLM were to be used, the challenges of model design would be increased. It is true, as noted above, that these are mitigated by the use of a lasso (or possibly other regularisation), but not eliminated.

Automation of such a model requires a selection of the basis functions mentioned in Section 6.2. It is necessary that the choice allow for interactions of all orders to be recognised in the model. As the number of potential covariates if the model increases, the number of interactions can mount very rapidly, possibly to the point of unworkability. This will sometimes necessitate the selection of interaction basis functions by the modeler, at which point erosion of the benefits of automated model design begins.

ANNs endeavour to address this situation. Their very general structure (see (8) to (10)) renders them sufficiently flexible to fit a data set usually as well as a GLM, and to identify and model dependencies in the data. They represent the ultimate in automation, since the user has little opportunity to intervene in feature selection.

However, this flexibility comes at a price. The output function of the ANN, from which the model values are fitted to data points, becomes abstract and inscrutable. While providing a forecast, the ANN may provide the user with little or no understanding of the data. This can be dangerous, as the user may lack control over extrapolation into the future (outside the span of the data) required for prediction.

The literature contains some recent attempts to improve on this situation with xNNs, which endeavor to provide some shape for the network's output function, and so render it physically meaningful. For example, the output function may be expressed in terms of basis functions parallel to those used for a lasso. However, experience with this form of lasso indicates that effort may still be required for interpretation of the model output expressed in this form.

In summary, the case is still to be made for both GMs and MLMs. Particular difficulties are embedded in GMs that may prove insurmountable. MLMs hold great promise but possibly require further development if they are to be fully domesticated and realise their loss-reserving potential.

A tantalising prospect is the combination of GMs and ANNs to yield the best of both worlds. To the author's knowledge, no such model has yet been formulated, but the vision might be the definition of a cascaded GM with one or more ANNs used to fit the sub-models or the connections between them, or both.

Funding: This research was funded by the Australian Research Council's Linkage Projects funding scheme, project number LP130100723.

Conflicts of Interest: The author declares no conflict of interest in the production of this research.

References

Ahlgren, Marcus. 2018. Claims Reserving Using Gradient Boosting and Generalized Linear Models. Master's thesis, KTH Royal Institute of Technology School of Engineering Sciences, Stockholm, Sweden. Available online: http://www.diva-portal.org/smash/record.jsf?pid=diva2%3A1215659&dswid=-4333 (accessed on 19 July 2019).

Antonio, K., and R. Plat. 2014. Micro-level stochastic loss reserving for general insurance. *Scandinavian Actuarial Journal* 2014: 649–69. [CrossRef]

Baxter, L. A., S. M. Coutts, and S. A. F. Ross. 1980. Applications of linear models in motor insurance. *Transaction of the 21st International Congress of Actuaries* 2: 11.

Brockman, M. J., and T. S. Wright. 1992. Statistical motor rating: Making effective use of your data. *Journal of the Institute of Actuaries* 119: 457–526. [CrossRef]

Fisher, W. H., and J. T. Lange. 1973. Loss reserve testing: A report year approach. *Proceedings of the Casualty Actuarial Society* 60: 189–207.

Gabrielli, A. 2019. A Neural Network Boosted Double OverDispersed Poisson Claims Reserving Model. Available online: https://ssrn.com/abstract=3365517 (accessed on 19 July 2019).

Gao, G., and S. Meng. 2018. Stochastic claims reserving via a Bayesian spline model with random loss ratio effects. *ASTIN Bulletin* 48: 55–88. [CrossRef]

Hachemeister, C. A. 1978. A structural model for the analysis of loss reserves. *Bulletin d'Association Royal des Actuaires Belges* 73: 17–27.

Hachemeister, C. A. 1980. A stochastic model for loss reserving. *Transactions of the 21st International Congress of Actuaries* 1: 185–94.

Hachemeister, C. A., and J. N. Stanard. 1975. *IBNR Claims Count Estimation with Static Lag Functions*. Arlington County: Casualty Actuarial Society.

Harej, B., R. Gächter, and S. Jamal. 2017. Individual Claim Development with Machine Learning. Report of the ASTIN Working Party of the International Actuarial Association. Available online: http://www.actuaries.org/ASTIN/Documents/ASTIN_ICDML_WP_Report_final.pdf (accessed on 19 July 2019).

Harvey, A. C. 1989. *Forecasting, Structural Time Series and the Kalman Filter*. Cambridge: Cambridge University Press.

Hesselager, O. 1994. A Markov Model for Loss Reserving. *Astin Bulletin* 24: 183–93. [CrossRef]

Huang, J., X. Wu, and X. Zhou. 2016. Asymptotic behaviors of stochastic reserving: Aggregate versus individual models. *European Journal of Operational Research* 249: 657–66. [CrossRef]

Jamal, S., S. Canto, R. Fernwood, C. Giancaterino, M. Hiabu, L. Invernizzi, T. Korzhynska, Z. Martin, and H. Shen. 2018. Machine Learning & Traditional Methods Synergy in Non-Life Reserving. Report of the ASTIN Working Party of the International Actuarial Association. Available online: https://www.actuaries.org/IAA/Documents/ASTIN/ASTIN_MLTMS%20Report_SJAMAL.pdf (accessed on 19 July 2019).

Kuo, K. 2018. DeepTriangle: A deep learning approach to loss reserving. *arXiv*.

Li, H., C. O'Hare, and F. Vahid. 2017. A flexible functional form approach to mortality modeling: Do we need additional cohort dummies? *Journal of Forecasting* 36: 357–67. [CrossRef]

McCullagh, P., and J. A. Nelder. 1989. *Generalized Linear Models*, 2nd ed. London: Chapman & Hall.

McGuire, G., G. Taylor, and H. Miller. 2018. Self-Assembling Insurance Claim Models Using Regularized Regression and Machine Learning. Available online: https://papers.ssrn.com/sol3/papers.cfm?abstract_id=3241906 (accessed on 19 July 2019).

Mack, T. 1993. Distribution-free calculation of the standard error of chain ladder reserve estimates. *ASTIN Bulletin* 23: 213–25. [CrossRef]

Miranda, M. D., J. P. Nielsen, and R. J. Verrall. 2013. Double chain ladder. *Astin Bulletin* 42: 59–76.

Meyers, G. G. 2015. *Stochastic Loss Reserving Using Bayesian MCMC Models*. CAS Monograph Series Number 1. Monograph Commissioned by the Casualty Actuarial Society; Arlington: Casualty Actuarial Society.

Meyers, G. G., and P. Shi. 2011. Loss Reserving Data Pulled from NAIC Schedule P. Available online: http://www.casact.org/research/index.cfm?fa=loss_reserves_data (accessed on 19 July 2019).

Mulquiney, P. 2006. Artificial Neural Networks in Insurance Loss Reserving. Paper Presented at the 9th Joint Conference on Information Sciences 2006—Proceedings, Kaohsiung, Taiwan, 8–11 October; Amsterdam: Atlantis Press. Available online: https://www.atlantis-press.com/search?q=mulquiney (accessed on 19 July 2019).

Nelder, J. A., and R. W. M. Wedderburn. 1972. Generalised linear models. *Journal of the Royal Statistical Society, Series A* 135: 370–84. [CrossRef]

Norberg, R. 1993. Prediction of outstanding liabilities in non-life insurance. *Astin Bulletin* 23: 95–115. [CrossRef]

Norberg, R. 1999. Prediction of outstanding liabilities II. Model extensions variations and extensions. *Astin Bulletin* 29: 5–25. [CrossRef]

Pigeon, M., K. Antonio, and M. Denuit. 2013. Individual loss reserving with the multivariate skew normal framework. *Astin Bulletin* 43: 399–428. [CrossRef]

Pigeon, M., K. Antonio, and M. Denuit. 2014. Individual loss reserving using paid–incurred data. *Insurance: Mathematics and Economics* 58: 121–31.

Reid, D. H. 1978. Claim reserves in general insurance. *Journal of the Institute of Actuaries* 105: 211–96. [CrossRef]

Taylor, G. 2000. *Loss Reserving: An Actuarial Perspective*. Dordrecht: Kluwer Academic Publishers.

Taylor, G. 2008. Second order Bayesian revision of a generalised linear model. *Scandinavian Actuarial Journal* 2008: 202–42. [CrossRef]

Taylor, G. 2011. Maximum likelihood and estimation efficiency of the chain ladder. *ASTIN Bulletin* 41: 131–55.

Taylor, G. C. 1986. *Claims Reserving in Non-Life Insurance*. Amsterdam: North-Holland.

Taylor, G., and M. Campbell. 2002. Statistical Case Estimation. Research Paper No. 104 of the Centre for Actuarial Studies. University of Melbourne. Available online: https://fbe.unimelb.edu.au/__data/assets/pdf_file/0009/2592072/104.pdf (accessed on 19 July 2019).

Taylor, G., and G. McGuire. 2004. Loss reserving with GLMs: A case study. Paper presented at the Spring 2004 Meeting of the Casualty Actuarial Society, Colorado Springs, CO, USA, May 16–19; pp. 327–92.

Taylor, G., and G. McGuire. 2009. Adaptive reserving using Bayesian revision for the exponential dispersion family. *Variance* 3: 105–30.

Taylor, G., and G. McGuire. 2016. *Stochastic Loss Reserving Using Generalized Linear Models*. CAS Monograph Series, Number 3, Monograph Commissioned by the Casualty Actuarial Society; Arlington: Casualty Actuarial Society.

Taylor, G., G. McGuire, and J. Sullivan. 2008. Individual claim loss reserving conditioned by case estimates. *Annals of Actuarial Science* 3: 215–56. [CrossRef]

Taylor, G., and P. Mulquiney. 2007. Modelling mortgage insurance as a multi-state process. *Variance* 1: 81–102.

Taylor, G., and J. Xu. 2016. An empirical investigation of the value of finalisation count information to loss reserving. *Variance* 10: 75–120. [CrossRef]

Tibshirani, R. 1996. Regression Shrinkage and Selection via the lasso. *Journal of the Royal Statistical Society, Series B (Methodological)* 58: 267–88. [CrossRef]

Tweedie, M. C. K. 1984. An index which distinguishes between some important exponential families. In *Statistics: Applications and New Directions, Proceedings of the Indian Statistical Golden Jubilee International Conference*. Edited by J. K. Ghosh and J. Roy. West Bengal: Indian Statistical Institute, pp. 579–604.

Vaughan, J., A. Sudjianto, E. Brahimi, J. Chen, and V. N. Nair. 2018. Explainable neural networks based on additive index models. *arXiv*.

Venter, G. G., and Ş. Şahın. 2018. Parsimonious parameterization of age-period-cohort models by Bayesian shrinkage. *ASTIN Bulletin* 48: 89–110. [CrossRef]

Wright, T. S. 1990. A stochastic method for claims reserving in general insurance. *Journal of the Institute of Actuaries* 117: 677–731. [CrossRef]

Wüthrich, M. V. 2018a. Neural networks applied to chain-ladder reserving. *European Actuarial Journal* 8: 407–36. [CrossRef]

Wüthrich, M. V. 2018b. Machine learning in individual claims reserving. *Scandinavian Actuarial Journal* 2018: 465–80. [CrossRef]

Wüthrich, M. V., and C. Buser. 2017. *Data Analytics for Non-Life Insurance Pricing*. Zurich: RiskLab Switzerland, Department of Mathematics, ETH Zurich.

Wüthrich, M. V., and M. Merz. 2008. *Stochastic Claim Reserving Methods in Insurance*. Chichester: John Wiley & Sons, Ltd.

© 2019 by the author. Licensee MDPI, Basel, Switzerland. This article is an open access article distributed under the terms and conditions of the Creative Commons Attribution (CC BY) license (http://creativecommons.org/licenses/by/4.0/).

MDPI
St. Alban-Anlage 66
4052 Basel
Switzerland
Tel. +41 61 683 77 34
Fax +41 61 302 89 18
www.mdpi.com

Risks Editorial Office
E-mail: risks@mdpi.com
www.mdpi.com/journal/risks

www.ingramcontent.com/pod-product-compliance
Lightning Source LLC
LaVergne TN
LVHW071959080526
838202LV00064B/6795